CAMBRIDGE  SCHOOL

Shakespeare

The
Winter's
Tale

Edited by Sheila Innes and Elizabeth Huddlestone

Series Editor: Rex Gibson
Director, Shakespeare and Schools Project

CAMBRIDGE
UNIVERSITY PRESS

CAMBRIDGE UNIVERSITY PRESS
Cambridge, New York, Melbourne, Madrid, Cape Town, Singapore, São Paulo

Cambridge University Press
The Edinburgh Building, Cambridge CB2 2RU, UK

www.cambridge.org
Information on this title: www.cambridge.org/9780521599559

First published 1999
5th printing 2006

Printed in the United Kingdom at the University Press, Cambridge

A catalogue record for this publication is available from the British Library

ISBN-10 978-0-521-59955-9 paperback
ISBN-13 0-521-59955-5 paperback

Prepared for publication by Stenton Associates
Designed by Richard Morris, Stonesfield Design
Picture research by Callie Kendall

'Autolycus' by Louis MacNeice on pages 108 and 110 is reprinted by permission of
David Higham Associates.

'Instructions to an Actor' by Edwin Morgan on pages 198 and 200 is reproduced from
Collected Poems by permission of Carcanet Press Limited.

Thanks are due to the following for permission to reproduce photographs:
Jacket foreground: detail of *Primavera* by Sandro Botticelli, c. 1478,
Uffizi/Bridgeman Art Library, London/New York; background: detail of *February*
by the Limbourg Brothers, Victoria & Albert Museum/Bridgeman Art Library,
London/New York. 14, by kind permission of the Marquess of Tavistock and the
Trustees of the Bedford Estate; 18*l*, 156, 196, Joe Cocks Studio Collection/photo:
Shakespeare Centre Library, Stratford-upon-Avon; 18*r*, Tom Holt Theatre Photo-
graphic Collection/photo: Shakespeare Centre Library, Stratford-upon-Avon; 35, 64,
130, 165, 217, Shakespeare Centre Library, Stratford-upon-Avon; 70, Robert Fludd:
Utrisque Cosmi Historia, 1617; 78, 98, 213, © Richard Kalina; 84, 211, Method &
Madness (photo: Simon Annand); 104, John Haynes; 148, The Bodleian Library,
University of Oxford, Ms. Douce. 332, f. 58*r* (detail); 164, Morris Newcombe; 170,
Richard Mildenhall/Arena Images; 203, Photograph by Angus McBean, Copyright
of the Harvard Theatre Collection, The Houghton Library.

Contents

Cambridge School Shakespeare

This edition of *The Winter's Tale* is part of the *Cambridge School Shakespeare* series. Like every other play in the series, it has been specially prepared to help all students in schools and colleges.

This *The Winter's Tale* aims to be different from other editions of the play. It invites you to bring the play to life in your classroom, hall or drama studio through enjoyable activities that will increase your understanding. Actors have created their different interpretations of the play over the centuries. Similarly, you are encouraged to make up your own mind about *The Winter's Tale*, rather than having someone else's interpretation handed down to you.

Cambridge School Shakespeare does not offer you a cut-down or simplified version of the play. This is Shakespeare's language, filled with imaginative possibilities. You will find on every left-hand page: a summary of the action, an explanation of unfamiliar words, and a choice of activities on Shakespeare's language, characters and stories.

Between each act and in the pages at the end of the play, you will find notes, illustrations and activities. These will help to increase your understanding of the whole play.

There are a large number of activities to give you the widest choice to suit your own particular needs. Please don't think you have to do every one. Choose the activities that help you most.

This edition will be of value to you whether you are studying for an examination, reading for pleasure, or thinking of putting on the play to entertain others. You can work on the activities on your own or in groups. Many of the activities suggest a particular group size, but don't be afraid to make up smaller or larger groups to suit your own purposes.

Although you are invited to treat *The Winter's Tale* as a play, you don't need special dramatic or theatrical skills to do the activities. By choosing your activities, and by exploring and experimenting, you can make your own interpretations of Shakespeare's language, characters and stories. Whatever you do, remember that Shakespeare wrote his plays to be acted, watched and enjoyed.

Rex Gibson

This edition of *The Winter's Tale* uses the text of the play established by Professor Susan Snyder in *The New Cambridge Shakespeare*.

List of characters

The Court of Sicilia

LEONTES	King of Sicilia
HERMIONE	Queen of Sicilia
MAMILLIUS	their son
PERDITA	their daughter
CAMILLO	
ANTIGONUS	} courtiers
CLEOMENES	
DION	
PAULINA	wife to Antigonus
EMILIA	lady in waiting
GAOLER	
MARINER	

Lords, ladies, gentlemen of the court, servants

TIME as chorus

The Court of Bohemia

POLIXENES	King of Bohemia
FLORIZEL	his son
ARCHIDAMUS	a courtier

The people of Bohemia

SHEPHERD	
CLOWN	the Shepherd's son
AUTOLYCUS	a thief
MOPSA	} shepherdesses
DORCAS	
SERVANT	to the Shepherd

Other shepherds and shepherdesses, twelve herdsmen
disguised as satyrs

The action of the play takes place in Sicilia and Bohemia.

I

Archidamus and Camillo discuss the long-standing friendship of their kings. The King of Sicilia is expected to visit Bohemia, and Archidamus fears the hospitality will not be as magnificent as in Sicilia.

1 Opening problems ... (in pairs)

It is always difficult for actors to get on stage in role – even more so at the beginning of the play. You have been asked to play the parts of Archidamus and Camillo.

* Decide where you have just come from.
* Improvise a short scene to lead into your first line on stage.
* Consider how close an adviser you might be to your respective kings.

2 Politeness run mad? (in pairs)

Archidamus believes that the Bohemians cannot hope to match the extent of the welcome extended by Sicilia when the return visit is paid. He goes so far as to suggest that they will drink or even drug the Sicilians into insensibility, so that the deficiencies of Bohemia cannot be judged.

* Try different ways of speaking this scene. Is Archidamus earnest, sardonic, joking ...? How does Camillo react?
* Remember this exchange as you read on, and consider whether it is meant to suggest a difference in sophistication between the two courts, or whether it is just an exaggerated way of praising the hospitality of the Sicilian court.

3 Tone of voice

What clues does Shakespeare give in the punctuation for the actor playing Archidamus about the way his lines should be spoken?

justified requited, absolved
in the freedom of my knowledge knowing it to be true
unintelligent unaware
insufficience inadequacies

Sicilia (line 17) Leontes, King of Sicilia
Bohemia (line 17) Polixenes, King of Bohemia
branch flourish (or, divide?)
attorneyed represented
vast huge distance

The Winter's Tale

ACT 1   SCENE 1
Sicilia: King Leontes' palace

Enter CAMILLO *and* ARCHIDAMUS

ARCHIDAMUS If you shall chance, Camillo, to visit Bohemia on the like
occasion whereon my services are now on foot, you shall see, as I
have said, great difference betwixt our Bohemia and your Sicilia.

CAMILLO I think this coming summer the King of Sicilia means to pay
Bohemia the visitation which he justly owes him.   5

ARCHIDAMUS Wherein our entertainment shall shame us: we will be
justified in our loves; for indeed –

CAMILLO Beseech you –

ARCHIDAMUS Verily, I speak it in the freedom of my knowledge: we
cannot with such magnificence, in so rare – I know not what to   10
say. We will give you sleepy drinks, that your senses, unintelligent
of our insufficience, may, though they cannot praise us, as little
accuse us.

CAMILLO You pay a great deal too dear for what's given freely.

ARCHIDAMUS Believe me, I speak as my understanding instructs me,   15
and as mine honesty puts it to utterance.

CAMILLO Sicilia cannot show himself over-kind to Bohemia. They
were trained together in their childhoods, and there rooted betwixt
them then such an affection which cannot choose but branch now.
Since their more mature dignities and royal necessities made   20
separation of their society, their encounters, though not personal,
hath been royally attorneyed with interchange of gifts, letters,
loving embassies; that they have seemed to be together, though
absent; shook hands, as over a vast; and embraced as it were from
the ends of opposed winds. The heavens continue their loves!   25

> *Archidamus and Camillo agree on the qualities of Leontes' son,*
> *Mamillius, saying that he makes everyone feel younger. Polixenes says*
> *he must return to Bohemia. Leontes asks him to stay longer.*

1 Protesting too much

Both Archidamus and Camillo use hyperbole (exaggerated language)
when describing Mamillius. Look back over the first scene and list the
images describing the affection between the two kings, and those
describing the qualities of the young prince. Suggest how these images
affect your first impression of the play.

2 The entrance of the court (in small groups)

In one production Archidamus and Camillo struggled to build a toy
fort in Scene 1 (giving the actors motivation, and accounting for the
occasional fragmentation of speech). The members of the court entered,
leading a blindfolded Mamillius. They applauded as the blindfold was
removed. While Mamillius and the courtiers played with his fort and
other toys, the conversation between the two kings took place. Visually
and symbolically this staging confirmed what had been said in Scene 1
about the importance of Mamillius. It also gave the silent actors on
stage a function to perform while the kings and queen spoke. Try as
many ways as you can of staging the entrance of the court, justifying
each.

3 'Nine changes of the wat'ry star' (in pairs)

Polixenes says he has been away from Bohemia for nine months. You
will find as you read on that time is an important theme in the play.
Speak lines 1–27, taking the roles of Polixenes and Leontes. Notice the
possible sexual undertones here, for example, nine months.

---

physics the subject is a tonic for
  every citizen
wat'ry star moon
a burden an occupant
for perpetuity/Go hence in debt
  be grateful to you for ever as we
  depart

cipher a symbol of increase
  (as in arithmetic)
questioned concerned
sneaping biting

4

ARCHIDAMUS I think there is not in the world either malice or matter
to alter it. You have an unspeakable comfort of your young prince
Mamillius. It is a gentleman of the greatest promise that ever
came into my note.

CAMILLO I very well agree with you in the hopes of him. It is a gallant   30
child; one that, indeed, physics the subject, makes old hearts
fresh. They that went on crutches ere he was born desire yet their
life to see him a man.

ARCHIDAMUS Would they else be content to die?

CAMILLO Yes, if there were no other excuse why they should desire to   35
live.

ARCHIDAMUS If the king had no son they would desire to live on
crutches till he had one.

Exeunt

ACT 1 SCENE 2
Sicilia: King Leontes' palace

Enter LEONTES, HERMIONE, MAMILLIUS, POLIXENES,
CAMILLO, and Attendants

POLIXENES Nine changes of the wat'ry star hath been
The shepherd's note since we have left our throne
Without a burden. Time as long again
Would be filled up, my brother, with our thanks,
And yet we should for perpetuity   5
Go hence in debt. And therefore, like a cipher,
Yet standing in rich place, I multiply
With one 'We thank you' many thousands more
That go before it.

LEONTES   Stay your thanks a while,
And pay them when you part.

POLIXENES   Sir, that's tomorrow.   10
I am questioned by my fears of what may chance
Or breed upon our absence, that may blow
No sneaping winds at home to make us say,
'This is put forth too truly'. Besides, I have stayed
To tire your royalty.

Polixenes refuses to stay any longer and Leontes asks Hermione to add her voice to his. Hermione assures Polixenes that all is well in Bohemia. Polixenes still refuses to stay longer.

---

1 Rehearsal techniques

Try different ways of speaking Hermione's speeches from lines 28–44, for example:

- walking around the room, changing direction at each punctuation mark
- with humour
- intimately
- sitting down to rest occasionally; she is in the late stages of her pregnancy.

Join with two other members of your class, to play Polixenes and Leontes, and see how your rehearsal techniques have helped your performance.

2 Echoes (in groups of three)

Take parts, and as Hermione speaks, Polixenes and Leontes echo all the powerful words that she uses; for example, 'drawn oaths', 'beat ...'. What do these words suggest about her character?

3 'We'll thwack him hence with distaffs!'

A distaff is the stick onto which wool was spun. Because spinning was a traditionally female activity, a distaff became a symbol of womanhood and domesticity. Hermione implies that if the reason that Polixenes does not want to leave is that he truly misses his son, she would, as a woman, encourage him to leave.

Make a list of alternative modern images you might use in a similar situation. Try to suggest equivalents which could symbolise femininity.

Very sooth in truth
I'll no gainsaying I will not take no for an answer
The bygone day proclaimed was given to us yesterday

ward position of defence
adventure/The borrow risk the loan
gest date
jar tick

LEONTES	We are tougher, brother, 15

Than you can put us to't.

POLIXENES	No longer stay.

LEONTES One sev'night longer.

POLIXENES	Very sooth, tomorrow.

LEONTES We'll part the time between's then; and in that
    I'll no gainsaying.

POLIXENES	Press me not, beseech you, so.

    There is no tongue that moves, none, none i'th'world 20
    So soon as yours could win me. So it should now,
    Were there necessity in your request, although
    'Twere needful I denied it. My affairs
    Do even drag me homeward; which to hinder
    Were, in your love, a whip to me, my stay 25
    To you a charge and trouble. To save both,
    Farewell, our brother.

LEONTES	Tongue-tied, our queen? Speak you.

HERMIONE I had thought, sir, to have held my peace until
    You had drawn oaths from him not to stay. You, sir,
    Charge him too coldly. Tell him you are sure 30
    All in Bohemia's well: this satisfaction
    The bygone day proclaimed. Say this to him,
    He's beat from his best ward.

LEONTES	Well said, Hermione.

HERMIONE To tell he longs to see his son were strong.
    But let him say so, then, and let him go; 35
    But let him swear so, and he shall not stay –
    We'll thwack him hence with distaffs!

[Leontes draws apart]

    Yet of your royal presence I'll adventure
    The borrow of a week. When at Bohemia
    You take my lord, I'll give him my commission 40
    To let him there a month behind the gest
    Prefixed for's parting; yet, good deed, Leontes,
    I love thee not a jar o'th'clock behind
    What lady she her lord. You'll stay?

POLIXENES	No, madam.

HERMIONE Nay, but you will?

POLIXENES	I may not, verily. 45

Hermione insists that Polixenes should stay longer, either as her prisoner or her guest. He agrees. Polixenes speaks of the boyhood innocence of himself and Leontes.

1 'My prisoner, or my guest?' (in pairs)

In line 53, 'pay your fees' refers to a common English practice in the fifteenth to eighteenth centuries. On release, prisoners, even if innocent, paid a fee to an officer such as the Sheriff or the gaoler.

Take parts as Polixenes and Hermione. Work on lines 51–60 to show how Hermione might use the prison/guest references to persuade Polixenes in her physical actions or expressions; for example, by pretending to handcuff him.

2 Original Sin (in pairs)

Polixenes' lines 67–75 refer to the doctrine of Original Sin. Traditional Christian belief says that because of the sins of Adam and Eve in the Garden of Eden, everyone carries some evil in them. Polixenes, using the image of the innocent lamb, says that if he and Leontes had continued throughout life behaving as they did when children, they would have been able to present themselves on the Day of Judgement as innocent of all crimes.

a Some people feel that Polixenes' final five words claim freedom from all sin, others that he is claiming that he could have been innocent except for the hereditary Original Sin. What is your interpretation?

b Talk together about whether you feel that children's play is naturally innocent, and about the effectiveness of the imagery that Polixenes uses.

---

limber vows weak promises
unsphere the stars knock the stars out of their normal courses
import offending imply some wrongdoing on my part

verier wag more mischievous
imposition cleared Original Sin forgiven

HERMIONE   Verily?
     You put me off with limber vows; but I,
     Though you would seek t'unsphere the stars with oaths,
     Should yet say, 'Sir, no going'. Verily,
     You shall not go; a lady's 'Verily' 's   50
     As potent as a lord's. Will you go yet?
     Force me to keep you as a prisoner,
     Not like a guest; so you shall pay your fees
     When you depart, and save your thanks. How say you?
     My prisoner, or my guest? By your dread 'Verily',   55
     One of them you shall be.
POLIXENES   Your guest then, madam:
     To be your prisoner should import offending,
     Which is for me less easy to commit
     Than you to punish.
HERMIONE   Not your gaoler then,
     But your kind hostess. Come, I'll question you   60
     Of my lord's tricks and yours when you were boys.
     You were pretty lordings then?
POLIXENES   We were, fair queen,
     Two lads that thought there was no more behind
     But such a day tomorrow as today,
     And to be boy eternal.
HERMIONE   Was not my lord   65
     The verier wag o'th'two?
POLIXENES   We were as twinned lambs that did frisk i'th'sun
     And bleat the one at th'other. What we changed
     Was innocence for innocence; we knew not
     The doctrine of ill-doing, nor dreamed   70
     That any did. Had we pursued that life,
     And our weak spirits ne'er been higher reared
     With stronger blood, we should have answered heaven
     Boldly, 'Not guilty', the imposition cleared
     Hereditary ours.
HERMIONE   By this we gather   75
     You have tripped since.

Hermione jokes with Polixenes that she and Polixenes' wife led to the end of innocence for him and Leontes. She tells Leontes that Polixenes will stay. Leontes recalls his wooing of Hermione.

1 The return of Leontes (in groups of three)

When precisely does Leontes rejoin Hermione and Polixenes? He must be there to speak at line 86. Try the effect of each of the following:
- he joins them at line 86
- he returns during line 82 and overhears their conversation
- having Hermione or Polixenes invite him to join their conversation.

Talk together about the different impressions each possibility might give to your audience. Explore how the different times of returning affect the way that Leontes speaks his line 'At my request he would not.' Does he say it slightly angrily, coldly, sarcastically, or ...? To whom would you have him speak this line – to the audience, to Hermione, or to a courtier, or ...?

2 'Cram's with praise' (in pairs)

Hermione's lines 90–100 are full of questions, apparently not giving time for Leontes to answer.

a Read her speech, taking turns to speak each question.

b One person speaks Hermione's lines while Leontes tries to get a word in edgeways!

c Change roles. While Hermione speaks her lines, Leontes refuses to answer.

d Share what you have learned from the three different ways of delivering this speech, which claims that praise needs to be spoken, and has long-lasting effects.

---

unfledged days childhood
Grace to boot! Heaven help us
Cram's fill us
ride's ride us (persuade us)
ere/With spur ... an acre before I could ride a short distance at full speed (punishment doesn't work!)

crabbèd bitter
clap thyself declare yourself (to 'clap hands' was to signal agreement to a contract)

POLIXENES   O my most sacred lady,
          Temptations have since then been born to's: for
          In those unfledged days was my wife a girl;
          Your precious self had then not crossed the eyes
          Of my young playfellow.
HERMIONE   Grace to boot!   80
          Of this make no conclusion, lest you say
          Your queen and I are devils. Yet go on;
          Th'offences we have made you do we'll answer,
          If you first sinned with us, and that with us
          You did continue fault, and that you slipped not   85
          With any but with us.
LEONTES   Is he won yet?
HERMIONE He'll stay, my lord.
LEONTES   At my request he would not.
          Hermione, my dearest, thou never spok'st
          To better purpose.
HERMIONE   Never?
LEONTES   Never but once.
HERMIONE What, have I twice said well? When was't before?   90
          I prithee tell me. Cram's with praise, and make's
          As fat as tame things. One good deed dying tongueless
          Slaughters a thousand waiting upon that.
          Our praises are our wages; you may ride's
          With one soft kiss a thousand furlongs ere   95
          With spur we heat an acre. But to th'goal:
          My last good deed was to entreat his stay.
          What was my first? It has an elder sister,
          Or I mistake you. O, would her name were Grace!
          But once before I spoke to th'purpose? When?   100
          Nay, let me have't; I long.
LEONTES   Why, that was when
          Three crabbèd months had soured themselves to death
          Ere I could make thee open thy white hand
          And clap thyself my love; then didst thou utter,
          'I am yours for ever.'
HERMIONE   'Tis Grace indeed.   105
          Why, lo you now, I have spoke to th'purpose twice:
          The one for ever earned a royal husband;
          Th'other for some while a friend.

*Leontes is suddenly jealous of the relationship between Hermione and
Polixenes, suspecting their every action. He wonders if Mamillius is
really his son and claims all women are deceitful.*

1 Leontes' jealousy

Leontes leaps from a mere suspicion to absolute conviction that
Hermione is having an affair with Polixenes. In Shakespeare's time it
was thought that people's blood mingled during sexual intercourse; 'to
mingle friendship far is mingling bloods.' (line 109). In Leontes' eyes
Hermione and Polixenes seem so friendly that he suspects they have
made love. His suspicion is so strong that his heart races: 'I have tremor
cordis on me.' (line 110).

a Many actors suggest that Hermione gives her hand to Polixenes at
   line 108, 'for some while a friend'. Where else do you think would
   be a suitable moment in lines 108–19 for them to take hands?

b Clearly Leontes is speaking an aside in lines 108–19, unheard by
   others on the stage. Work out in detail how he delivers his lines
   (to whom? movement and gestures? tone? and so on).

c Men whose wives were adulterous were called cuckolds, and they
   were represented in art and literature as having horns on their
   foreheads. Such men were considered figures of fun for not being
   able to control their wives. Identify each reference to horned
   animals opposite: deer, neat (cattle), heifer, calf, shoots (horns).
   Suggest an action Leontes might make at each mention.

d What are Hermione and Polixenes doing to give Leontes a motive
   for jealousy?

mort death	**o'er-dyed blacks** clothes re-dyed
I'fecks! in faith	black (false)
bawcock fine fellow	**bourn** boundary
virginalling/Upon his palm	**welkin** sky blue
playing on his hand (like a piano)	**My collop!** piece of my flesh (chip
rough pash and the shoots bull's	off the old block)
shaggy head and horns	**dam** mother

LEONTES [*Aside*]   Too hot, too hot!
          To mingle friendship far is mingling bloods.
          I have tremor cordis on me: my heart dances,
          But not for joy, not joy. This entertainment
          May a free face put on, derive a liberty
          From heartiness, from bounty, fertile bosom,
          And well become the agent – 't may, I grant;
          But to be paddling palms and pinching fingers,
          As now they are, and making practised smiles
          As in a looking-glass, and then to sigh, as 'twere
          The mort o'th'deer – O, that is entertainment
          My bosom likes not, nor my brows. – Mamillius,
          Art thou my boy?
MAMILLIUS   Ay, my good lord.
LEONTES   I'fecks!
          Why, that's my bawcock. What, hast smutched thy nose?
          They say it is a copy out of mine. Come, captain,
          We must be neat – not neat, but cleanly, captain.
          And yet the steer, the heifer and the calf
          Are all called neat. Still virginalling
          Upon his palm? – How now, you wanton calf,
          Art thou my calf?
MAMILLIUS   Yes, if you will, my lord.
LEONTES Thou want'st a rough pash and the shoots that I have
          To be full like me. Yet they say we are
          Almost as like as eggs. Women say so,
          That will say anything. But were they false
          As o'er-dyed blacks, as wind, as waters, false
          As dice are to be wished by one that fixes
          No bourn 'twixt his and mine, yet were it true
          To say this boy were like me. Come, sir page,
          Look on me with your welkin eye. Sweet villain!
          Most dear'st! My collop! Can thy dam? May't be?

Handwritten marginalia:
She had more power than he could get P. to stay.
Son is contaminated I thought you were mine but women lie

Line numbers: 110, 115, 120, 125, 130, 135

Leontes is increasingly disturbed by jealousy and his expression is noticed by Polixenes and Hermione. Leontes denies feeling upset. He says looking at Mamillius reminds him of his own childhood.

1 Searching out the meaning

Everyone finds lines 138–46 difficult to understand. The incoherence indicates Leontes' state of mind. It also explains Polixenes' line, 'What means Sicilia?' One interpretation is: 'Passion influences everything, even dreams – which are not real. So passion is very likely to affect reality ('something') violently and that is proved by my own reaction of jealousy.'

Suggest other possible interpretations, and how you would advise an actor to deliver the lines.

Leontes remembers a favourite gown of his – 'unbreeched, in my green velvet coat'. At the time this picture of John Russell was painted (1623) all small children, boys and girls, wore frocks.

2 'Take eggs for money' (in pairs)

In line 161, Leontes' question means 'will you take something of little value instead of cash?' or 'will you allow yourself to be cheated?'. Talk together about Leontes' relationship with Mamillius at this moment, and how to stage it.

Affection passion, lust
coactive collaborating with
credent believable
commission expectation
kernel nut

squash unripe peapod/child
happy man be's dole! may he be lucky
parasite favourite

Affection, thy intention stabs the centre.
Thou dost make possible things not so held,
Communicat'st with dreams – how can this be? –   140
With what's unreal thou coactive art,
And fellow'st nothing. Then 'tis very credent
Thou mayst co-join with something; and thou dost,
And that beyond commission, and I find it,
And that to the infection of my brains   145
And hard'ning of my brows.   *insanity*

POLIXENES   What means Sicilia?
HERMIONE He something seems unsettled.
POLIXENES   How, my lord?
LEONTES What cheer? How is't with you, best brother?
HERMIONE   You look
As if you held a brow of much distraction.
Are you moved, my lord?
LEONTES   No, in good earnest.   150
How sometimes nature will betray its folly,
Its tenderness, and make itself a pastime
To harder bosoms! Looking on the lines
Of my boy's face, methoughts I did recoil
Twenty-three years, and saw myself unbreeched,   155
In my green velvet coat; my dagger muzzled,
Lest it should bite its master and so prove,
As ornaments oft do, too dangerous.
How like, methought, I then was to this kernel,
This squash, this gentleman. Mine honest friend,   160
Will you take eggs for money?   *will you be deceived*
MAMILLIUS No, my lord, I'll fight.
LEONTES You will? Why, happy man be's dole! My brother,
Are you so fond of your young prince as we
Do seem to be of ours?
POLIXENES   If at home, sir   165
He's all my exercise, my mirth, my matter;
Now my sworn friend, and then mine enemy;
My parasite, my soldier, statesman, all.
He makes a July's day short as December,
And with his varying childness cures in me   170
Thoughts that would thick my blood.

*Leontes asks Hermione to show welcome to Polixenes. When they have
gone he speaks of his certainty that they are having an affair, and
imagines the world full of unfaithful wives.*

1 Alter ego (in pairs)

Leontes appears to be allowing Hermione to behave towards Polixenes
exactly as he doesn't want her to behave.

a Speak lines 171–80 ('So stands … the sky.') with both of you
taking the roles of Leontes, one speaking the lines of the script,
and the other voicing his thoughts as his other self, or alter ego.

b Next, speak lines 171–85 with Leontes' alter ego directing, to find
the most effective way of conveying the character's feelings.

2 Imagery in a jealous mind

In lines 180–207, striking images suggest the state of Leontes' mind.

line 180 angling – playing them deliberately on a (fishing) line
line 183 holds up the neb – holding up her mouth (beak) as
though to be kissed
line 186 Inch-thick, knee-deep – wading more deeply into sin
line 186 a forked one! – with the horns of a cuckold
line 187 plays – sexual misbehaviour
line 188 Play – take a role in a play
line 189 hiss – be jeered at because the role he plays is shameful
line 190 knell – bell rung at death or funeral
lines 194–5 sluiced/pond fished – contemptuous sexual images
(spoken to the audience?)
line 201 bawdy planet – indecent planet (Venus)
line 204 barricado – barricade or defence

Speak the lines, emphasising Leontes' disgust through the sound of
the words.

Officed performing the same
function
graver more serious
Apparent to my heart heir to my
love

bents inclinations
arms her takes his arm
cuckolds husbands with unfaithful
wives
Physic medicine

LEONTES   So stands this squire
          Officed with me. We two will walk, my lord,
          And leave you to your graver steps. Hermione,
          How thou lov'st us show in our brother's welcome.
          Let what is dear in Sicily be cheap.   175
          Next to thyself and my young rover, he's
          Apparent to my heart.
HERMIONE   If you would seek us,
          We are yours i'th' garden. Shall's attend you there?   *He wants them to be together — prove his?*
LEONTES To your own bents dispose you; you'll be found,
          Be you beneath the sky. [*Aside*] I am angling now,   *prove his?* 180
          Though you perceive me not how I give line.
          Go to, go to!
          How she holds up the neb, the bill to him!
          And arms her with the boldness of a wife
          To her allowing husband!

          [*Exeunt Polixenes, Hermione, and Attendants*]

                         Gone already!   185
          Inch-thick, knee-deep, o'er head and ears a forked one!
          Go play, boy, play: thy mother plays, and I
          Play too – but so disgraced a part whose issue   *shame*
          Will hiss me to my grave. Contempt and clamour
          Will be my knell. Go play, boy, play. There have been,   190
          Or I am much deceived, cuckolds ere now;
          And many a man there is, even at this present,
          Now, while I speak this, holds his wife by th'arm,
          That little thinks she has been sluiced in's absence,
          And his pond fished by his next neighbour, by   195
          Sir Smile, his neighbour. Nay, there's comfort in't
          Whiles other men have gates, and those gates opened,
          As mine, against their will. Should all despair   *Women are*
          That have revolted wives, the tenth of mankind   *Revolting.*
          Would hang themselves. Physic for't there's none: 200
          It is a bawdy planet, that will strike
          Where 'tis predominant; and 'tis powerful, think it,
          From east, west, north and south. Be it concluded,
          No barricado for a belly. Know't,
          It will let in and out the enemy   205
          With bag and baggage. Many thousand on's
          Have the disease and feel't not. How now, boy!

Leontes sends Mamillius to play. He fears everyone is gossiping about him, and asks Camillo if the ordinary people know why Polixenes has decided to stay longer in Sicilia.

a 'I am like you, they say.'   b 'Why, that's some comfort.'

1 Jealousy

Leontes' jealousy has progressed swiftly and has corrupted every aspect of his thoughts. It affects not only his view of Hermione and Polixenes, but also Camillo and the rest of the court. He thinks that everyone must have noticed, and be laughing at him.

a Try speaking lines 221–8 as one long sneer. Then decide whether that is an appropriate style for Leontes to use on stage.

b How might Camillo react?

They're here with me already
 everyone can see what's going on
rounding whispering in corners
gust hear
pate head

For thy conceit … blocks
 you can understand things more
 quickly than stupid people
severals … extraordinary
 individuals of outstanding
 intelligence
Lower messes lower-class people

flag

MAMILLIUS I am like you, they say.
LEONTES   Why, that's some comfort.
        What, Camillo there?
CAMILLO Ay, my good lord.   210

                    [*He comes forward*]

LEONTES Go play, Mamillius; thou'rt an honest man.

                                    [*Exit Mamillius*]

        Camillo, this great sir will yet stay longer.
CAMILLO You had much ado to make his anchor hold;
        When you cast out, it still came home.
LEONTES   Didst note it?
CAMILLO He would not stay at your petitions – made   *rejection*   215
        His business more material.
LEONTES   Didst perceive it?
        [*Aside*] They're here with me already, whisp'ring, rounding,
        'Sicilia is a so-forth.' 'Tis far gone
        When I shall gust it last. – How cam't, Camillo,   *He loves it*
        That he did stay?   *not Him –*
CAMILLO   At the good queen's entreaty.   220
LEONTES 'At the queen's' be't. 'Good' should be pertinent,
        But so it is, it is not. Was this taken
        By any understanding pate but thine?
        For thy conceit is soaking, will draw in
        More than the common blocks. Not noted, is't,   225
        But of the finer natures? By some severals
        Of head-piece extraordinary? Lower messes
        Perchance are to this business purblind? Say.
CAMILLO Business, my lord? I think most understand
        Bohemia stays here longer.
LEONTES   Ha?
CAMILLO   Stays here longer.   230
LEONTES Ay, but why?
CAMILLO To satisfy your highness, and the entreaties
        Of our most gracious mistress.

Leontes accuses Camillo of being dishonest or foolishly not seeing things as they are, and of betraying his trust. Camillo asks to be shown what he has done wrong.

1 'Satisfy' (in pairs)

Leontes' questioning of Camillo's choice of words shows how obsessed he is by his jealousy. Camillo intends to suggest that Polixenes stayed to please ('satisfy') Leontes and Hermione. Leontes' paranoia immediately interprets the word 'satisfy' in its sexual sense.

Take turns to speak lines 233–41, emphasising at least one word in each line with which Leontes intends to insult or cause pain to Camillo.

2 Camillo

You are the actor playing Camillo. The director has asked you to make some notes towards the preparation work on your character. Concentrate particularly on lines 250–64 where Camillo, feeling he is unjustly accused, gives himself a kind of character reference. Consider the following questions:

- how old are you?
- how long have you been with Leontes?
- what do you look like?
- what is your bearing?
- what kind of voice do you have?
- what has Leontes confided in you?
- what kind of costume do you think you might wear?
- how do you defend yourself in lines 250–64 against the charge of being negligent, foolish and fearful?

---

chamber-counsels private affairs
priest-like as a priest hearing confession
hoxes honesty behind puts a hobble (restraint) on honesty

grafted implanted
rich stake drawn big prize won
my trespass … visage how my mistake appears, what I've done wrong

LEONTES   Satisfy?
            Th'entreaties of your mistress? Satisfy?
            Let that suffice. I have trusted thee, Camillo,   235
            With all the nearest things to my heart, as well   *I so trusted*
            My chamber-counsels, wherein, priest-like, thou   *you*
            Hast cleansed my bosom, I from thee departed   *password*
            Thy penitent reformed. But we have been
            Deceived in thy integrity, deceived //   240
            In that which seems so.
CAMILLO   Be it forbid, my lord!
LEONTES To bide upon't: thou art not honest; or,
            If thou inclin'st that way, thou art a coward,
            Which hoxes honesty behind, restraining
            From course required; or else thou must be counted   245
            A servant grafted in my serious trust
            And therein negligent; or else a fool
            That see'st a game played home, the rich stake drawn,
            And tak'st it all for jest.
CAMILLO   My gracious lord,
            I may be negligent, foolish, and fearful;   250
            In every one of these no man is free,
            But that his negligence, his folly, fear,
            Among the infinite doings of the world,
            Sometime puts forth. In your affairs, my lord,
            If ever I were wilful-negligent,   255
            It was my folly; if industriously
            I played the fool, it was my negligence,
            Not weighing well the end; if ever fearful
            To do a thing where I the issue doubted,
            Whereof the execution did cry out   260
            Against the non-performance, 'twas a fear
            Which oft infects the wisest. These, my lord,
            Are such allowed infirmities that honesty
            Is never free of. But, beseech your grace,
            Be plainer with me, let me know my trespass   265
            By its own visage; if I then deny it,
            'Tis none of mine.

Leontes says Camillo must know that Hermione is unfaithful.
Camillo denies she is false. Leontes gives precise details of the basis for his
suspicions of Hermione and Polixenes.

1 Can't you see what's happening?
(whole class, large space)

Walk around the room speaking Leontes' lines 267–78 and 284–96.
Make a very definite change in direction each time there is a punctuation
mark. When you have finished, find a partner and compare notes about
what this exercise has told you about Leontes' state of mind.

2 Puppets act it out! (groups of three)

Lines 284–92 give details of what Leontes' jealousy leads him to
imagine. Use two of the members of the group as Leontes' puppets.
The actor playing Leontes directs the other two to act out his imagined
suspicions.

3 'Slippery'

In line 273, Leontes cannot bring himself to say the word 'unfaithful'
about Hermione. Make a list of other words he might have in his mind
but cannot speak.

4 'Nothing' (in pairs)

Shakespeare knew that repetition of a word could greatly enhance
mood and dramatic effect. For Leontes, if Hermione is unfaithful then
the whole world is nothing. Work together on lines 292–6 trying to find
the most effective way of delivering the repeated 'nothing'.

---

eye-glass lens of your eye
cogitation the ability to think
  straight
hobby-horse loose woman
flax-wench peasant

puts to has sex
troth-plight solemn promise to
  marry
'Shrew curse (beshrew)
pin and web cataract
betimes at once, quickly

LEONTES   Ha' not you seen, Camillo –
              But that's past doubt, you have, or your eye-glass
              Is thicker than a cuckold's horn – or heard –
              For to a vision so apparent rumour   270
              Cannot be mute – or thought – for cogitation
              Resides not in that man that does not think –
              My wife is slippery? If thou wilt confess,
              Or else be impudently negative,
              To have nor eyes, nor ears, nor thought, then say   275
              My wife's a hobby-horse, deserves a name
              As rank as any flax-wench that puts to
              Before her troth-plight: say't, and justify't.
CAMILLO I would not be a stander-by to hear
              My sovereign mistress clouded so without   280
              My present vengeance taken. 'Shrew my heart,
              You never spoke what did become you less
              Than this; which to reiterate were sin
              As deep as that, though true.
LEONTES   Is whispering nothing?
              Is leaning cheek to cheek? Is meeting noses?   285
              Kissing with inside lip? Stopping the career
              Of laughter with a sigh? – a note infallible
              Of breaking honesty – Horsing foot on foot?
              Skulking in corners? Wishing clocks more swift?
              Hours, minutes? Noon, midnight? And all eyes   290
              Blind with the pin and web but theirs – theirs only,
              That would unseen be wicked? Is this nothing?
              Why then the world and all that's in't is nothing,
              The covering sky is nothing, Bohemia nothing,
              My wife is nothing, nor nothing have these nothings,   295
              If this be nothing.
CAMILLO   Good my lord, be cured
              Of this diseased opinion, and betimes,
              For 'tis most dangerous.
LEONTES   Say it be, 'tis true.
CAMILLO No, no, my lord.

Leontes curses and insults Camillo for doubting him. He asks Camillo to poison Polixenes. Camillo cannot believe that Hermione is unchaste, but Leontes insists his own troubled view is the right one.

1 Imagery (in pairs)

Compare Leontes' imagery on the page opposite with that on page 17. You will see that here too it is both visual and graphic. He has progressed from his first thoughts that Hermione and Polixenes may have kissed, to doubting even whether Mamillius is his son. Taking the roles of Camillo and Leontes, speak the lines on the facing page several times. Then identify the images Leontes uses, setting out your list in the same style as that on page 16.

2 Euphemism (in pairs)

A euphemism is a word or phrase that people use instead of saying something which they find embarrassing. Leontes uses 'a lasting wink' (line 317) as a euphemism for death. Make a list of other words or phrases commonly used for death, for example, 'passed away'. Suggest why people frequently use euphemisms for certain topics, such as death or sex.

3 Camillo's dilemma

Camillo is in a 'Catch 22' situation. Whatever he does, he cannot win. If he disobeys Leontes, he will lose Leontes' patronage. If he obeys, which as a loyal subject he ought to do, he will become a murderer. Make a guess at what Camillo will do to resolve his dilemma. As you read on, check the accuracy of your guess.

---

hovering temporiser indecisive timeserver
glass hourglass
bare eyes had true sight
thrifts gains
benched ... worship raised to higher position at table
galled injured
draught drink
cordial medicinal
rash quick acting
crack flaw
blench delude himself, be inconstant

LEONTES   It is; you lie, you lie.
         I say thou liest, Camillo, and I hate thee,   300
         Pronounce thee a gross lout, a mindless slave,
         Or else a hovering temporiser that
         Canst with thine eyes at once see good and evil,
         Inclining to them both. Were my wife's liver
         Infected as her life, she would not live   305
         The running of one glass.
CAMILLO   Who does infect her?
LEONTES Why, he that wears her like her medal, hanging
         About his neck, Bohemia; who, if I
         Had servants true about me that bare eyes
         To see alike mine honour as their profits,   310
         Their own particular thrifts, they would do that
         Which should undo more doing. Ay, and thou
         His cupbearer, whom I from meaner form
         Have benched and reared to worship, who mayst see
         Plainly as heaven sees earth and earth sees heaven,   315
         How I am galled, mightst bespice a cup
         To give mine enemy a lasting wink;
         Which draught to me were cordial.
CAMILLO   Sir, my lord,
         I could do this, and that with no rash potion,
         But with a ling'ring dram that should not work   320
         Maliciously, like poison. But I cannot
         Believe this crack to be in my dread mistress,
         So sovereignly being honourable.
         I have loved thee –
LEONTES   Make that thy question, and go rot!
         Dost think I am so muddy, so unsettled,   325
         To appoint myself in this vexation,
         Sully the purity and whiteness of my sheets –
         Which to preserve is sleep, which being spotted
         Is goads, thorns, nettles, tails of wasps –
         Give scandal to the blood o'th'prince, my son –   330
         Who I do think is mine, and love as mine –
         Without ripe moving to't? Would I do this?
         Could man so blench?

> *Camillo agrees to kill Polixenes, insisting that Leontes should act lovingly towards Hermione. Leontes agrees. Once alone, Camillo says that he cannot kill Polixenes. Polixenes returns, puzzled.*

1 Camillo's subtext

Camillo is deeply unhappy at Leontes' accusations. His words 'fetch off Bohemia' (line 334) seem to Leontes to mean, 'I will kill Polixenes'. But 'fetch off' can also mean rescue. If this is what Camillo really means, his line, 'Account me not thy servant' may have a double meaning too.

Shakespeare uses this technique of double meaning or subtext in many other plays. For example, in *Romeo and Juliet*, Act 3 Scene 5, lines 67–123, Juliet speaks to her mother of her love for Romeo but uses language that seems to say she hates him.

Consider what Camillo's thoughts might be between lines 333 and 347. Remember that he has sworn an oath of allegiance to Leontes, and the king was considered to be God's representative on earth. What might he mean when he says, 'I must believe you' (line 333), and his final two lines 346–7 to Leontes?

2 Camillo makes up his mind

Lines 351–64 are a soliloquy. The convention of soliloquies is that when a character is speaking alone on stage, he or she speaks the truth.

Imagine you are auditioning for the role of Camillo. Learn his soliloquy and perform it to the rest of the group. Look back at page 20 to help you in your preparation.

---

for sealing … tongues stopping gossip
countenance as clear guiltless expression
keep with remain friendly with
case difficult situation

in rebellion … so too since he is rebelling against his own true sane nature, he expects his followers to do likewise
brass … stone … parchment records engraved on brass or stone, or written on parchment
To me a break-neck death to me
warp twist, distort

CAMILLO   I must believe you, sir.
    I do; and will fetch off Bohemia for't –
    Provided that when he's removed your highness   335
    Will take again your queen as yours at first,
    Even for your son's sake, and thereby for sealing
    The injury of tongues in courts and kingdoms
    Known and allied to yours.
LEONTES   Thou dost advise me
    Even so as I mine own course have set down.   340
    I'll give no blemish to her honour, none.
CAMILLO My lord,
    Go then; and with a countenance as clear
    As friendship wears at feasts, keep with Bohemia
    And with your queen. I am his cupbearer;   345
    If from me he have wholesome beverage,
    Account me not your servant.
LEONTES   This is all.
    Do't and thou hast the one half of my heart;
    Do't not, thou split'st thine own.
CAMILLO   I'll do't, my lord.
LEONTES I will seem friendly, as thou hast advised me.   *Exit*   350
CAMILLO O miserable lady! But, for me,
    What case stand I in? I must be the poisoner
    Of good Polixenes, and my ground to do't
    Is the obedience to a master – one
    Who, in rebellion with himself, will have   355
    All that are his so too. To do this deed,
    Promotion follows. If I could find example
    Of thousands that had struck anointed kings
    And flourished after, I'd not do't; but since
    Nor brass, nor stone, nor parchment bears not one,   360
    Let villainy itself forswear't. I must
    Forsake the court; to do't or no is certain
    To me a break-neck. Happy star reign now!
    Here comes Bohemia.

Enter POLIXENES

POLIXENES   This is strange: methinks
    My favour here begins to warp. Not speak?   365
    Good day, Camillo.

Polixenes says that Leontes has looked at him contemptuously.
Camillo seems reluctant to explain what has happened, but Polixenes
demands to be told.

---

1 An offstage meeting (in pairs)

Use lines 368–75 to improvise this short offstage meeting between
Leontes and Polixenes. Just what was Leontes' facial expression?
('Wafting his eyes to th'contrary' may mean avoiding eye contact; and
'such a contenance/As ... himself' suggests that Leontes looks as if he
had lost a valuable and much loved area of land.)

2 'Dare not' (in pairs)

Take parts and speak lines 376 and 377. Then turn away and without
stopping write for two minutes any thoughts that come into your head.
Then, repeat the two lines. How has this 'stream of consciousness'
exercise changed the way that you say them? Read your notes to your
partner and see if this makes a difference to a third speaking of the
lines.

3 The basilisk

In line 388, when Polixenes says, 'Make me not sighted like the
basilisk', he is referring to a mythical monster. The basilisk, sometimes
called a cockatrice, was able to kill with just a look or a breath. It was
supposed to be hatched by a serpent from a cock's egg. Suggest why
Polixenes uses this image of the basilisk at this moment.

---

customary compliment usual
  greeting
breeding going on
Be intelligent to me tell me what
  you know
A party in this alteration an
  accomplice
sped the better got on, thrived

thereto ... experienced having
  gained that position through
  education
In whose success ... gentle
  from whom we inherit the status
  of gentlemen
does behove which is important for
In ignorant concealment and
  leave me in ignorance

CAMILLO   Hail, most royal sir!
POLIXENES What is the news i'th'court?
CAMILLO   None rare, my lord.
POLIXENES The king hath on him such a countenance
    As he had lost some province, and a region
    Loved as he loves himself. Even now I met him   370
    With customary compliment, when he,
    Wafting his eyes to th'contrary, and falling
    A lip of much contempt, speeds from me, and
    So leaves me to consider what is breeding
    That changes thus his manners.   375
CAMILLO I dare not know, my lord.
POLIXENES How, dare not? Do not? Do you know, and dare not?
    Be intelligent to me. 'Tis thereabouts;
    For, to yourself what you do know, you must,
    And cannot say you dare not. Good Camillo,   380
    Your changed complexions are to me a mirror
    Which shows me mine changed too; for I must be
    A party in this alteration, finding
    Myself thus altered with't.
CAMILLO   There is a sickness
    Which puts some of us in distemper, but   385
    I cannot name the disease, and it is caught
    Of you, that yet are well.
POLIXENES   How, Caught of me?
    Make me not sighted like the basilisk.
    I have looked on thousands who have sped the better
    By my regard, but killed none so. Camillo,   390
    As you are certainly a gentleman, thereto
    Clerk-like experienced, which no less adorns
    Our gentry than our parents' noble names,
    In whose success we are gentle, I beseech you,
    If you know aught which does behove my knowledge   395
    Thereof to be informed, imprison't not
    In ignorant concealment.

Polixenes insists Camillo tell him what is wrong. Camillo says he has been ordered to kill Polixenes because Leontes thinks that Polixenes has been adulterous with Hermione. Polixenes is appalled.

1 'I must be answered' (in groups of three)

Camillo is torn between loyalty towards Leontes and honesty towards Polixenes.

Improvise a short scene where two friends have to give bad news involving a third friend. For example, her boyfriend has been seen with another girl. Before performing, try these two exercises:

- One person stands in the centre of the room. You do not know whether to give bad news to two friends. Each tries to persuade you. Give the answers 'I may not answer' or 'I will tell you' according to the strength of their persuasion.
- Make a list of alternative arguments to tell or not to tell.

2 Judas: the betrayer (in pairs)

Polixenes says that if he had done what Leontes suspects he would deserve his name to be linked with 'his that did betray the Best' – Judas Iscariot, who betrayed Jesus in the New Testament. In the *Inferno*, Dante writes of an imaginary vision of Hell where all the punishments are graded according to the nature of the sin. In the very lowest circle of Hell are placed the worst sinners: Judas, who betrayed Christ, and Brutus and Cassius, who betrayed Julius Caesar. Talk together about whether you feel betrayal of a friend is the worst sin.

3 'A sickness caught of me' (in pairs)

Using pages 29 and 31, make a note of all the words concerned with smell, disease, infection, adultery and jealousy. Decide how this list of words helps you to understand Polixenes' reactions.

---

conjure urge
suit appeal
incidency likelihood
savour foul smell

dullest most insensitive
continue … his body maintain his delusion as long as he lives

CAMILLO   I may not answer.
POLIXENES A sickness caught of me, and yet I well?
             I must be answered. Dost thou hear, Camillo,
             I conjure thee, by all the parts of man   400
             Which honour does acknowledge, whereof the least
             Is not this suit of mine, that thou declare
             What incidency thou dost guess of harm
             Is creeping toward me; how far off, how near;
             Which way to be prevented, if to be;   405
             If not, how best to bear it.
CAMILLO   Sir, I will tell you,
             Since I am charged in honour, and by him
             That I think honourable. Therefore mark my counsel,
             Which must be ev'n as swiftly followed as
             I mean to utter it, or both yourself and me   410
             Cry lost, and so good night.
POLIXENES   On, good Camillo.
CAMILLO I am appointed him to murder you.
POLIXENES By whom, Camillo?
CAMILLO   By the king.
POLIXENES   For what?
CAMILLO He thinks, nay with all confidence he swears,
             As he had seen't, or been an instrument   415
             To vice you to't, that you have touched his queen
             Forbiddenly.
POLIXENES   O then my best blood turn
             To an infected jelly, and my name
             Be yoked with his that did betray the Best!
             Turn then my freshest reputation to   420
             A savour that may strike the dullest nostril
             Where I arrive, and my approach be shunned,
             Nay, hated too, worse than the great'st infection
             That e'er was heard or read!
CAMILLO   Swear his thought over
             By each particular star in heaven and   425
             By all their influences, you may as well
             Forbid the sea for to obey the moon
             As or by oath remove or counsel shake
             The fabric of his folly, whose foundation
             Is piled upon his faith, and will continue   430
             The standing of his body.

Camillo says that he and Polixenes must flee Sicilia that night. Polixenes' followers should leave secretly in groups. Polixenes speaks of Leontes' power and Hermione's worthiness.

1 'I saw his heart in's face' (in pairs)

Polixenes has observed Leontes' 'lip of much contempt' (line 373), and now realises what this means. But do a person's intentions show in his or her face? In *Macbeth*, King Duncan says, 'There's no art to find the mind's construction in the face' about an unexpected traitor. On the other hand, in *Julius Caesar*, Caesar says of someone he mistrusts, 'Yon Cassius has a lean and hungry look.'

Discuss the idea that it is possible to read someone's character and thoughts just by looking at them, and judging by appearance.

2 Divided emotions (in pairs)

The ending of this act gives opportunities to the actors to show the conflict between wanting to stay in Sicilia and needing to leave quickly. Polixenes twice asks Camillo to go: 'Come, Camillo' and 'Let us avoid'. Camillo asks Polixenes to hurry: 'take the urgent hour. Come, sir, away!'.

Take parts and speak lines 460 to the end of the scene. Try acting out the lines to show the feeling of being pulled two ways. Then, still in role as Polixenes and Camillo, say what your feelings are at this moment of leaving.

this trunk my body
impawned as a pledge
posterns back gates
thy places ... mine your position will always be next to me

Professed declared friendship
Good expedition may a quick departure
ill-tane ill-founded
avoid depart

POLIXENES   How should this grow?

CAMILLO I know not; but I am sure 'tis safer to
   Avoid what's grown than question how 'tis born.
   If therefore you dare trust my honesty,
   That lies enclosèd in this trunk, which you   435
   Shall bear along impawned, away to-night!
   Your followers I will whisper to the business,
   And will by twos and threes, at several posterns,
   Clear them o'th'city. For myself, I'll put
   My fortunes to your service, which are here   440
   By this discovery lost. Be not uncertain,
   For, by the honour of my parents, I
   Have uttered truth; which if you seek to prove,
   I dare not stand by; nor shall you be safer
   Than one condemned by the king's own mouth,   445
   Thereon his execution sworn.

POLIXENES   I do believe thee:
   I saw his heart in's face. Give me thy hand.
   Be pilot to me, and thy places shall
   Still neighbour mine. My ships are ready, and
   My people did expect my hence departure   450
   Two days ago. This jealousy
   Is for a precious creature; as she's rare
   Must it be great; and as his person's mighty
   Must it be violent; and as he does conceive
   He is dishonoured by a man which ever   455
   Professed to him, why, his revenges must
   In that be made more bitter. Fear o'ershades me.
   Good expedition be my friend and comfort
   The gracious queen, part of his theme, but nothing
   Of his ill-tane suspicion. Come, Camillo,   460
   I will respect thee as a father if
   Thou bear'st my life off hence. Let us avoid.

CAMILLO It is in mine authority to command
   The keys of all the posterns. Please your highness
   To take the urgent hour. Come, sir, away!   465

            Exeunt

Looking back at Act 1
Activities for groups or individuals

1 Mamillius

Step into the role of director of a stage production and give your answers to the following questions:

- how old is Mamillius?
- how might an adult actor play the part?
- how might Mamillius react to his father's questioning of him during Scene 2 between lines 119–62?
- how would you keep a child actor involved and occupied when he is on stage, but not part of the main action?

2 Stage directions

When *The Winter's Tale* was first printed in 1623 it included only a few stage directions. Nearly all the stage directions in modern editions are the additions of later editors of the play. Such additions are printed in square brackets in this edition.

Although the original stage direction at the end of Scene 1 is '*Exeunt*' (all leave), Camillo immediately returns in Scene 2, and there is no real need to dispense with Archidamus. The actors playing these roles have asked your advice. What do you suggest that they do?

3 Camillo's autobiography

In Scene 2, lines 313–14, Leontes says that he has raised Camillo from 'meaner form' and promoted him to a position of respect. He also claims to have confided in Camillo things that should really have been confessed to a priest (lines 235–9). Remind yourself of all Camillo says in Act 1, and of Activity 2 on page 20, and write the chapter of Camillo's autobiography describing how he came to be Leontes' chief courtier.

4 Archidamus: a Bohemian courtier's story

Archidamus never appears in the play again after Scene 1, but he probably fled with Polixenes and Camillo in the ship that carried them away from Leontes' murderous intentions. Write his diary entry telling what he knows of the events in Act 1.

5 Leontes' jealousy

Working in large groups, stage the following series of tableaux to show the sequence of Leontes' jealousy during Scene 2:

- the whole court at line 87: 'At my request he would not.'
- Leontes, Hermione, and Polixenes at line 115–17
- the exit of Hermione, Polixenes and attendants at line 185
- Leontes, Mamillius and Camillo at line 207.

Leontes, Polixenes, Hermione. Which line do you think is being spoken at this moment in Scene 2?

Hermione asks her ladies to play with Mamillius.
The ladies remark on the imminent birth of the baby. Hermione calls
Mamillius back to tell her a story.

1 '… he so troubles me' (in groups of four)

What is Mamillius doing that 'so troubles' Hermione? Rehearse two or three entrances, and show them to the rest of the class. Discuss the atmosphere you wish to create. Remember the descriptions of Mamillius and his behaviour in Act 1 and build from these. There is little point in making him thoroughly obnoxious because it wouldn't fit with the rest of the play.

2 A forward child (in groups of three)

Practise lines 2–18 two or three times taking turns to play Mamillius. What is the reaction of the ladies to his comments about their appearance? Decide what you think was Shakespeare's dramatic intention in this short domestic exchange.

3 'Rounds apace'

How pregnant is Hermione? Both ladies comment on the visible signs of her pregnancy, and the second lady wishes Hermione an easy labour. Many of Shakespeare's audience would be well aware of the potential dangers of pregnancy, even for noble women. In Britain, in the sixteenth and seventeenth centuries, an average of 25 women per 1000 died in childbirth, compared with 0.12 per 1000 in the late twentieth century.

---

prince royal child
 (of either gender)
wanton play

Good time encounter her! may
she have a successful labour

ACT 2 SCENE 1

Sicilia: Hermione's room in the palace

Enter HERMIONE, MAMILLIUS, and LADIES

HERMIONE Take the boy to you; he so troubles me
    'Tis past enduring.

1 LADY   Come, my gracious lord,
    Shall I be your playfellow?

MAMILLIUS   No, I'll none of you.

1 LADY Why, my sweet lord?

MAMILLIUS You'll kiss me hard, and speak to me as if   5
    I were a baby still. I love you better.

2 LADY And why so, my lord?

MAMILLIUS   Not for because
    Your brows are blacker; yet black brows, they say,
    Become some women best, so that there be not
    Too much hair there, but in a semi-circle,   10
    Or a half-moon, made with a pen.

2 LADY   Who taught ' this?

MAMILLIUS I learned it out of women's faces. Pray now,
    What colour are your eyebrows?

1 LADY   Blue, my lord.

MAMILLIUS Nay, that's a mock. I have seen a lady's nose
    That has been blue, but not her eyebrows.

1 LADY   Hark ye,   15
    The queen your mother rounds apace. We shall
    Present our services to a fine new prince
    One of these days, and then you'd wanton with us,
    If we would have you.

2 LADY   She is spread of late
    Into a goodly bulk. Good time encounter her!   20

HERMIONE What wisdom stirs amongst you? Come, sir, now
    I am for you again. Pray you sit by us,
    And tell's a tale.

MAMILLIUS   Merry or sad shall't be?

HERMIONE As merry as you will.

Mamillius begins to whisper his story to his mother. Leontes questions the lords about the hasty disappearance of Polixenes and Camillo from court. He says that Camillo betrayed him.

1 'A sad tale's best for winter'

Presumably Mamillius is telling his story during the conversation between Leontes and the lord. Write the outline of the story told by Mamillius.

2 Director's decision!

What are the ladies doing during lines 30–55? Do they observe Leontes and curtsy? Do they sew or read? Or play soft music? If your acting space is small you will have some difficulty organising the set so that the queen and her child can speak together, but the ladies cannot hear Mamillius or Leontes. Sketch a floor plan for your acting space, and add the stage directions for the actions that you have devised for the ladies.

3 'I have drunk, and seen the spider'

Leontes' powerful image of the spider (lines 39–45) comes partly from the Elizabethan myth that spiders were poisonous – but only if seen. Give a similar example from your own experience where seeing an insect (or slug) in your own food or drink has made you feel ill.

4 Reacting to Leontes (in small groups)

One person speaks Leontes' lines 36–53, with the lords grouped around him. Direct sections of the speech to individual lords, each of whom has to react appropriately. Talk together about how the reactions can make the speech more dramatically effective for an audience.

Yond crickets Those chattering ladies
train servants, attendants
scour hurry
just censure correct judgement
Alack, … knowledge! I would be happier if I knew less

so blest! correct
gorge throat
hefts retching
pander go-between, pimp
pinched tortured
very trick … will puppet for them to manipulate

MAMILLIUS   A sad tale's best for winter. I have one   25
      Of sprites and goblins.
HERMIONE   Let's have that, good sir.
      Come on, sit down; come on, and do your best
      To fright me with your sprites; you're powerful at it.
MAMILLIUS   There was a man –
HERMIONE   Nay, come sit down; then on.
MAMILLIUS   Dwelt by a churchyard – I will tell it softly;   30
      Yond crickets shall not hear it.
HERMIONE   Come on, then,
      And give't me in mine ear.

          [*Enter* LEONTES, ANTIGONUS, *and* LORDS]

LEONTES   Was he met there? His train? Camillo with him?
LORD   Behind the tuft of pines I met them. Never
      Saw I men scour so on their way. I eyed them   35
      Even to their ships.
LEONTES   How blest am I
      In my just censure, in my true opinion!
      Alack, for lesser knowledge! How accursed
      In being so blest! There may be in the cup
      A spider steeped, and one may drink, depart,   40
      And yet partake no venom, for his knowledge
      Is not infected; but if one present
      Th'abhorred ingredient to his eye, make known
      How he hath drunk, he cracks his gorge, his sides,
      With violent hefts. I have drunk, and seen the spider.   45
      Camillo was his help in this, his pander.
      There is a plot against my life, my crown.
      All's true that is mistrusted. That false villain
      Whom I employed was pre-employed by him.
      He has discovered my design, and I   50
      Remain a pinched thing; yea, a very trick
      For them to play at will. How came the posterns
      So easily open?
LORD   By his great authority,
      Which often hath no less prevailed than so
      On your command.
LEONTES   I know't too well.   55

In front of all his retinue, Leontes accuses Hermione of being pregnant by Polixenes and sends Mamillius away. Hermione says that Leontes is mistaken.

1 'What is this? Sport?'

Leontes picks up Hermione's word 'sport', and uses it back to her to suggest a more sinister meaning of sexual games with Polixenes. You will find that he frequently re-interprets her words over their next exchanges.

Perhaps Hermione is so far from suspecting what Leontes thinks that she assumes that he has started a teasing game.

How might she say line 58? Try speaking her four words teasingly, fearfully, angrily, puzzled, and in other ways you can think of.

2 Insulting Hermione (in small groups)

Leontes speaks lines 64–78 to the lords, but the criticisms are all directed at Hermione. To understand how this might affect Hermione, try the following exercise: stand in a circle with one person in the centre as Hermione. Work through Leontes' speech, each person speaking one short section to Hermione. Make it as insulting as possible. Take it in turns to be in the middle as Hermione. Afterwards, compare your experience of how it feels to be accused, and what the exercise has helped you understand about Leontes' state of mind.

---

nayward contrary
without-door form external
 appearance

petty brands small indications
calumny slander
replenished complete

[*To Hermione*] Give me the boy. I am glad you did not
nurse him;
Though he does bear some signs of me, yet you
Have too much blood in him.

HERMIONE   What is this? Sport?

LEONTES Bear the boy hence; he shall not come about her.
Away with him, and let her sport herself   60
With that she's big with; for 'tis Polixenes
Has made thee swell thus.

[*Exit Mamillius with Attendants*]

HERMIONE   But I'd say he had not,
And I'll be sworn you would believe my saying,
Howe'er you lean to th'nayward.

LEONTES   You, my lords,
Look on her, mark her well: be but about   65
To say 'She is a goodly lady' and
The justice of your hearts will thereto add
''Tis pity she's not honest, honourable.'
Praise her but for this her without-door form,
Which on my faith deserves high speech, and straight   70
The shrug, the hum or ha, these petty brands
That calumny doth use – O, I am out!
That mercy does, for calumny will sear
Virtue itself – these shrugs, these hums and ha's,
When you have said she's goodly, come between,   75
Ere you can say 'she's honest'. But be't known,
From him that has most cause to grieve it should be,
She's an adultress.

HERMIONE   Should a villain say so,
The most replenished villain in the world,
He were as much more villain. You, my lord,   80
Do but mistake.

41

Leontes alleges that Hermione has committed adultery with Polixenes.
He accuses Camillo of being her associate in treachery. Hermione denies
all the accusations and appeals to the lords to judge her.

1 Deny the accusations (in pairs)

Take parts as Leontes and Hermione. Leontes speaks lines 81–95,
pausing at the end of each sense unit for Hermione to say, 'No, by my
life'. Afterwards suggest how this exercise adds to Hermione's feeling
of helplessness. At this point no one else on stage speaks in her defence.

2 Imagery of the Cosmos

Lines 100–7 contain two images from beliefs about the universe in
Shakespeare's time . When Leontes says, 'The centre is not big enough
to bear/A schoolboy's top', his image comes from the idea that the
Earth was the centre of the Universe.

   When Hermione says that 'some ill planet reigns', she is expressing
the belief that particular planets (for example, Mars and Saturn) have
an evil influence which is strongest when the planets are in the
ascendant. (See page 70 for a related picture.)

3 'The king's will be performed!'

Line 115 echoes the Lord's prayer ('Thy will be done'). During the
time that Shakespeare was writing many people considered the king to
be God's representative on earth. To defy the king was to defy God.
Do you think that Hermione is behaving as the ideal wife, protesting
her innocence but submitting to Leontes' will. Or is she using the word
'king' to refer to God? Suggest what you think Hermione means when
she says, 'The king's will be performed!'.

A fedary an associate
vulgars common people
privy/To knowing of
scarce can right me hardly make
  it up to me

He … speaks anyone who defends
  her is guilty just by speaking
measure me judge me

LEONTES   You have mistook, my lady,
          Polixenes for Leontes. O thou thing,
          Which I'll not call a creature of thy place,
          Lest barbarism, making me the precedent,
          Should a like language use to all degrees   85
          And mannerly distinguishment leave out
          Betwixt the prince and beggar. I have said
          She's an adultress; I have said with whom.
          More, she's a traitor, and Camillo is
          A fedary with her, and one that knows   90
          What she should shame to know herself
          But with her most vile principal – that she's
          A bed-swerver, even as bad as those
          That vulgars give bold'st titles; ay, and privy
          To this their late escape.
HERMIONE   No, by my life,   95
          Privy to none of this. How will this grieve you,
          When you shall come to clearer knowledge, that
          You thus have published me! Gentle my lord,
          You scarce can right me throughly then to say
          You did mistake.
LEONTES   No; if I mistake   100
          In those foundations which I build upon,
          The centre is not big enough to bear
          A schoolboy's top. Away with her to prison!
          He who shall speak for her is afar off guilty
          But that he speaks.
HERMIONE   There's some ill planet reigns.   105
          I must be patient till the heavens look
          With an aspect more favourable. Good my lords,
          I am not prone to weeping, as our sex
          Commonly are; the want of which vain dew
          Perchance shall dry your pities: but I have   110
          That honourable grief lodged here which burns
          Worse than tears drown. Beseech you all, my lords,
          With thoughts so qualified as your charities
          Shall best instruct you, measure me; and so
          The king's will be performed!
LEONTES   Shall I be heard?   115

Hermione asks for her women to be with her in prison to assist her.
Antigonus and the other lords try to defend her honour, saying some
villain has deceived Leontes.

1 'Adieu, my lord' (in pairs)

Take turns to speak Hermione's lines 116–24, exploring different
tones of voice. What does her speech add to your understanding of
Hermione?

2 Antigonus defends Hermione

Antigonus reacts strongly to Leontes' treatment of Hermione. He says
that if Hermione is an adulteress, then no woman can be trusted. He
tells Leontes that some 'putter-on' has deceived him, and swears that
he will castrate his own three young daughters if Hermione is guilty.
Speak Antigonus' speeches on the opposite page, then write a short
note advising an actor on how to deliver his lines.

3 'The queen is spotless ...' (in small groups)

The lords and Antigonus are silent when Hermione is present. Once
she has gone Leontes hardly manages to get a word in as his courtiers
defend Hermione's innocence. Why is there this difference? Talk
together about possible dramatic reasons. Does Shakespeare want to
emphasise Hermione's helplessness? Were the lords too stunned to
speak earlier? Or ...?

4 'Co-heirs'

Line 148 refers to the English laws of primogeniture, under which the
eldest son inherited his dead parents' whole estate. Where there were
no sons, all daughters shared the inheritance equally.

---

plight condition (pregnancy)
in couples chained together in
 pairs (like hounds)
dram fragment
land-damn thrash, laudanum
 (drug), curse throughout the land

geld/glib castrate
false generations illegitimate
 children
fair issue legitimate children

HERMIONE Who is't that goes with me? Beseech your highness
   My women may be with me, for you see
   My plight requires it. Do not weep, good fools:
   There is no cause. When you shall know your mistress
   Has deserved prison, then abound in tears   120
   As I come out. This action I now go on
   Is for my better grace. Adieu, my lord.
   I never wished to see you sorry; now
   I trust I shall. My women, come; you have leave.
LEONTES Go, do our bidding; hence!   125

    [*Exeunt Hermione, guarded, and Ladies*]

LORD Beseech your highness, call the queen again.
ANTIGONUS Be certain that you do, sir, lest your justice
   Prove violence, in the which three great ones suffer –
   Yourself, your queen, your son.
LORD   For her, my lord,
   I dare my life lay down, and will do't, sir,   130
   Please you t'accept it, that the queen is spotless
   I'th'eyes of heaven and to you – I mean
   In this which you accuse her.
ANTIGONUS   If it prove
   She's otherwise, I'll keep my stables where
   I lodge my wife; I'll go in couples with her;   135
   Than when I feel and see her, no farther trust her;
   For every inch of woman in the world,
   Ay, every dram of woman's flesh is false,
   If she be.
LEONTES   Hold your peaces.
LORD   Good my lord –
ANTIGONUS It is for you we speak, not for ourselves.   140
   You are abused, and by some putter-on
   That will be damned for't. Would I knew the villain –
   I would land-damn him! Be she honour-flawed,
   I have three daughters: the eldest is eleven,
   The second and the third, nine and some five;   145
   If this prove true, they'll pay for't! By mine honour,
   I'll geld 'em all; fourteen they shall not see
   To bring false generations. They are co-heirs,
   And I had rather glib myself than they
   Should not produce fair issue.

Leontes accuses the lords of not believing him and resorts to using his royal power, threatening to dismiss them. He rebukes Antigonus for not seeing what was obvious.

---

1 'Our prerogative' (in groups of three)

Leontes claims that his prerogative (the absolute rights and privileges of the sovereign) means that he has no need of his courtiers' advice, because a king's view of 'truth' must be right. Speak all the lines on the facing page several times, changing roles for each read-through. Afterwards, decide:

- why Leontes changes from the personal 'I' to the impersonal royal 'we'. In one of your readings try stressing Leontes' words 'we'/'our'/'us'.

- what gestures and actions the actor playing Leontes might make. For example, at line 153 some productions have Leontes strike Antigonus' face on 'thus'. One production even had Leontes stab Antigonus' hand with a dagger at that moment.

2 Leontes' evidence?

Leontes admits at line 177 that he has no visual evidence of the guilt of Hermione and Polixenes. Make a list of the 'evidence' Leontes thinks he has of Hermione's misconduct.

The instruments my fingers
dungy vile, base
this ground this matter
forceful instigation driving urges and insights
or stupefied/Or seeming so either stupid or pretending to be

overture disclosure, public action
gross obvious
touched conjecture came near a proof
nought for approbation nothing else for proof

LEONTES   Cease, no more!   150
   You smell this business with a sense as cold
   As is a dead man's nose; but I do see't and feel't,
   As you feel doing thus, and see withal
   The instruments that feel.
ANTIGONUS   If it be so,
   We need no grave to bury honesty: 155
   There's not a grain of it the face to sweeten
   Of the whole dungy earth.
LEONTES   What! Lack I credit?
LORD   I had rather you did lack than I, my lord,
   Upon this ground; and more it would content me
   To have her honour true than your suspicion,   160
   Be blamed for't how you might.
LEONTES   Why, what need we
   Commune with you of this, but rather follow
   Our forceful instigation? Our prerogative
   Calls not your counsels, but our natural goodness
   Imparts this; which if you, or stupefied   165
   Or seeming so in skill, cannot or will not
   Relish a truth like us, inform yourselves
   We need no more of your advice. The matter,
   The loss, the gain, the ord'ring on't, is all
   Properly ours.
ANTIGONUS   And I wish, my liege,   170
   You had only in your silent judgement tried it,
   Without more overture.
LEONTES   How could that be?
   Either thou art most ignorant by age,
   Or thou wert born a fool. Camillo's flight,
   Added to their familiarity –   175
   Which was as gross as ever touched conjecture,
   That lacked sight only, nought for approbation
   But only seeing, all other circumstances
   Made up to th'deed – doth push on this proceeding.

Leontes announces that he has sent to the sacred temple of Apollo at Delphi for confirmation of his suspicions. Antigonus comments ironically on Leontes' words. In Scene 2, Paulina visits the prison.

1 Why?

Leontes has sent his messengers, Cleomenes and Dion, to the god Apollo's temple at Delphi where they will be able to gain judgement on Hermione's supposed adultery (see page 72 for further information about the oracle). Leontes needs public confirmation that he is correct in his accusation of his wife. Although he is certain he is right, he says that the 'spiritual counsel' from the oracle 'Shall stop or spur' him.

a Identify in lines 189–96 the reasons Leontes gives for sending to the oracle, and the reason he gives for imprisoning Hermione.

b In line 197, Leontes says that he will speak in public to calm the fears of the people. Write the speech that he intends to make.

2 'Well done, my lord'

The lord has already shown his loyalty to Hermione in lines 129–30: 'For her, my lord,/I dare my life lay down'. But he is a subject of Leontes, and has only just been threatened with dismissal.

Try as many different ways as you can of saying line 188 to Leontes, for example, sarcastically, approvingly, under your breath, and so on.

3 He's making a fool of himself (in pairs)

Antigonus' aside at lines 198–9 shows clearly that he thinks Leontes' actions are foolish. Take parts as Antigonus and Paulina, and improvise the scene where he reports to his wife what has happened between Hermione and Leontes.

---

wild impetuous
in post in haste
Of stuffed sufficiency are extremely able

spiritual counsel had judgement received
confined removed, imprisoned

Yet, for a greater confirmation –   180
For in an act of this importance 'twere
Most piteous to be wild – I have dispatched in post
To sacred Delphos, to Apollo's temple,
Cleomenes and Dion, whom you know
Of stuffed sufficiency. Now, from the oracle   185
They will bring all, whose spiritual counsel had
Shall stop or spur me. Have I done well?

LORD Well done, my lord.

LEONTES Though I am satisfied, and need no more
Than what I know, yet shall the oracle   190
Give rest to th'minds of others, such as he,
Whose ignorant credulity will not
Come up to th'truth. So have we thought it good
From our free person she should be confined,
Lest that the treachery of the two fled hence   195
Be left her to perform. Come, follow us;
We are to speak in public, for this business
Will raise us all.

ANTIGONUS [*Aside*]   To laughter, as I take it,
If the good truth were known.

                                                           Exeunt

ACT 2   SCENE 2
Sicilia: a prison

Enter PAULINA, a GENTLEMAN, and Attendants

PAULINA The keeper of the prison, call to him.
Let him have knowledge who I am.

                                        [*Exit Gentleman*]

                                        Good lady,
No court in Europe is too good for thee;
What dost thou then in prison?

The Gaoler refuses to allow Paulina to visit the queen but agrees to bring out one of her ladies, Emilia, who tells Paulina that Hermione has had a baby daughter.

1 Paulina *versus* the Gaoler (in pairs)

Act out the exchange between Paulina and the Gaoler in lines 4–18. How does she try to persuade him to do what she wants? Try an aggressive approach, then perhaps a quieter one with some sarcasm. Which is more effective? As a director you might want to have some humour in this scene as a contrast to what Hermione is experiencing in prison.

2 Overhearing a conversation

When the Gaoler returns with Emilia, how near to them does he dare to stand in order to overhear? Advise him, with reasons.

3 Hermione's ordeal

Using the words from the page opposite which refer to Hermione, *either* write a short poem describing Hermione's feelings during the days of her imprisonment, *or* write a poem from Hermione to her new-born daughter under the title 'My poor prisoner'.

---

express commandment precise
 orders
no stain a stain purity a dishonour

colouring belief
Lusty healthy

[Enter GENTLEMAN, *with the* GAOLER*]*

       Now, good sir,
You know me, do you not?
GAOLER   For a worthy lady,   5
And one who much I honour.
PAULINA   Pray you, then,
Conduct me to the queen.
GAOLER   I may not, madam;
To the contrary I have express commandment.
PAULINA Here's ado,
To lock up honesty and honour from   10
Th'access of gentle visitors! Is't lawful, pray you,
To see her women? Any of them? Emilia?
GAOLER So please you, madam,
To put apart these your attendants, I
Shall bring Emilia forth.
PAULINA   I pray now, call her.   15
Withdraw yourselves.

    [Exeunt Gentleman and Attendants]

GAOLER   And, madam,
I must be present at your conference.
PAULINA Well, be't so, prithee.

          [Exit Gaoler]

Here's such ado to make no stain a stain
As passes colouring.

    [Enter GAOLER *with* EMILIA*]*

       Dear gentlewoman,   20
How fares our gracious lady?
EMILIA As well as one so great and so forlorn
May hold together. On her frights and griefs –
Which never tender lady hath borne greater –
She is, something before her time, delivered.   25
PAULINA A boy?
EMILIA   A daughter, and a goodly babe,
Lusty, and like to live. The queen receives
Much comfort in't; says, 'My poor prisoner,
I am innocent as you.'

Paulina promises to criticise sharply the king's mad behaviour.
She offers to take the child to him, hoping that the sight of the baby will
make him change his mind.

1 What is Paulina like? (in pairs)

When she describes the sharp-tongued way in which she will speak to
Leontes, Paulina refers to two traditions. First, in popular folk-tales,
the tongues of liars and cheats were supposed to blister – 'let my tongue
blister ...'. Second, a herald preceding a servant bringing an angry
message was traditionally dressed in red – 'red-looked anger'.

Each person speaks Paulina's lines 29–42. Then talk together about
the imagery she uses and what it suggests about her character.

2 Silence is golden (in pairs)

Recall times from your own experience when silence 'Persuades when
speaking fails' (line 42) – when your silence has been more effective
than giving voice to your thoughts and feelings.

3 'Please you ...'

To whom do you feel line 55 is addressed? Decide whether you think
it is to Paulina, the Gaoler or perhaps an attendant. Justify your
decision.

4 Will she succeed?

Do you think Paulina will be successful in her appeal to Leontes? Make
a guess about what will happen, and check the accuracy of your
judgement as you read on.

---

lunes madness
beshrew blast, curse
office duty
free undertaking generous offer

thriving issue successful outcome
meet suitable
hammered of this design was
   giving serious thought to this idea

PAULINA   I dare be sworn.
These dangerous, unsafe lunes i'th'king, beshrew them!   30
He must be told on't, and he shall. The office
Becomes a woman best; I'll take't upon me.
If I prove honey-mouthed, let my tongue blister,
And never to my red-looked anger be
The trumpet any more. Pray you, Emilia,   35
Commend my best obedience to the queen.
If she dares trust me with her little babe,
I'll show't the king, and undertake to be
Her advocate to th'loud'st. We do not know
How he may soften at the sight o'th'child: 40
The silence often of pure innocence
Persuades when speaking fails.
EMILIA   Most worthy madam,
Your honour and your goodness is so evident
That your free undertaking cannot miss
A thriving issue. There is no lady living   45
So meet for this great errand. Please your ladyship
To visit the next room, I'll presently
Acquaint the queen of your most noble offer,
Who but today hammered of this design,
But durst not tempt a minister of honour   50
Lest she should be denied.
PAULINA   Tell her, Emilia,
I'll use that tongue I have; if wit flow from't
As boldness from my bosom, let't not be doubted
I shall do good.
EMILIA   Now be you blest for it!
I'll to the queen. Please you come something nearer.   55

Paulina successfully argues for the baby's freedom. In Scene 3, Leontes regrets that Polixenes is out of reach. He feels that the execution of Hermione would calm him. A servant reports that Mamillius is ill.

1 More than my job's worth! (in pairs)

When Paulina argues for the baby's freedom, the Gaoler tries to stick precisely to his instructions for fear of punishment.

a Write a letter from the Gaoler to his wife describing his important prisoner and his attitude to her and the baby, Paulina's visit and his dilemma.

b Improvise a modern scene, where you are able to persuade a reluctant official of your point of view.

2 'Nor night nor day no rest' (in small groups)

Leontes believes that his peace of mind will return only when Hermione and Polixenes are both dead. He can't kill Polixenes because he is beyond his aim: 'out of the blank/And level of my brain'. So his jealousy prompts him to 'hook' Hermione to him and have her burnt. Burning was a common punishment for heretics and witches, but not for adulterous queens. Leontes' feelings about Hermione are as violent as Othello's about Desdemona: 'I'll chop her into messes.'

a Leontes is thinking agitatedly about the situation. Explore different ways of speaking lines 1–9, then step into role as directors and advise the actor how he might deliver the lines (for example, pacing? smoking? head in hands? looking at Hermione's portrait? or …?).

b Discuss other instances where jealousy has driven someone to consider extreme revenge.

---

pass it let it out of prison
in being still living
harlot king Polixenes
beyond mine arm out of my
  reach

blank centre of the target, bull's
  eye (archery)
level aim or range
moiety part

GAOLER Madam, if't please the queen to send the babe,
        I know not what I shall incur to pass it,
        Having no warrant.
PAULINA   You need not fear it, sir.
        This child was prisoner to the womb, and is
        By law and process of great nature thence   60
        Freed and enfranchised; not a party to
        The anger of the king, nor guilty of –
        If any be – the trespass of the queen.
GAOLER I do believe it.
PAULINA Do not you fear; upon mine honour, I   65
        Will stand betwixt you and danger.

                                            Exeunt

ACT 2   SCENE 3
Sicilia: King Leontes' palace

Enter LEONTES

LEONTES Nor night nor day no rest. It is but weakness
         To bear the matter thus, mere weakness. If
         The cause were not in being – part o'th'cause,
         She, th'adultress; for the harlot king
         Is quite beyond mine arm, out of the blank   5
         And level of my brain, plot-proof; but she
         I can hook to me – say that she were gone,
         Given to the fire, a moiety of my rest
         Might come to me again. Who's there?

                [Enter a SERVANT]

SERVANT   My lord?
LEONTES How does the boy?
SERVANT   He took good rest tonight.   10
         'Tis hoped his sickness is discharged.

Leontes says that Mamillius' illness is related to the shame of Hermione. He thinks that Polixenes and Camillo mock him in Bohemia. Paulina criticises those who try to prevent her entering.

1 Leontes' feelings (in pairs)

Shakespeare often uses lists, piling up item on item to increase dramatic intensity. In lines 14–17, he lists at least eight of Mamillius' symptoms.

Speak Leontes' lines 12–26 several times, taking one sentence each, then respond to each of the following:

- Does Leontes speak lines 12–17 to the servant or in soliloquy?
- Who do you think is 'him' (line 18)?
- What do lines 18–26 suggest about Leontes' state of mind?
- Prepare a set of notes which a director might give to the actor playing Leontes to help his performance of these lines.

2 Enter Paulina – with difficulty (in small groups)

When Paulina enters with the baby, the servant, her husband and the other lords try to prevent her. Leontes seems not to hear the conversation because at line 39 he asks, 'What noise there, ho?'.

a Practise several ways of staging Paulina's entrance, thinking particularly about possible actions and gestures, and about what effects you are trying to achieve.

b Is it really likely that Leontes is unaware of Paulina's entrance and her criticism of his attendants? Work out what Leontes might do between lines 26 and 39 that reveals more of his character.

Conceiving understanding
be second to me give me your
  support
free innocent
needless heavings unnecessary
  sighs

purge him of that humour
  cleanse him of that grief
  (see page 71 for information on the
  humours)

LEONTES To see his nobleness!
　　　　Conceiving the dishonour of his mother,
　　　　He straight declined, drooped, took it deeply,
　　　　Fastened and fixed the shame on't in himself;   15
　　　　Threw off his spirit, his appetite, his sleep,
　　　　And downright languished. Leave me solely. Go,
　　　　See how he fares.   [*Exit Servant*]
　　　　　　　　　　Fie, fie, no thought of him!
　　　　The very thought of my revenges that way
　　　　Recoil upon me – in himself too mighty,   20
　　　　And in his parties, his alliance. Let him be
　　　　Until a time may serve. For present vengeance,
　　　　Take it on her. Camillo and Polixenes
　　　　Laugh at me, make their pastime at my sorrow.
　　　　They should not laugh if I could reach them, nor   25
　　　　Shall she, within my power.

Enter PAULINA [*carrying a baby, followed by* ANTIGONUS,
LORDS, and SERVANT]

LORD   You must not enter.
PAULINA Nay, rather, good my lords, be second to me.
　　　　Fear you his tyrannous passion more, alas,
　　　　Than the queen's life? A gracious, innocent soul,
　　　　More free than he is jealous.
ANTIGONUS   That's enough.   30
SERVANT Madam, he hath not slept tonight, commanded
　　　　None should come at him.
PAULINA   Not so hot, good sir;
　　　　I come to bring him sleep. 'Tis such as you,
　　　　That creep like shadows by him and do sigh
　　　　At each his needless heavings, such as you   35
　　　　Nourish the cause of his awaking. I
　　　　Do come with words as med'cinal as true,
　　　　Honest as either, to purge him of that humour
　　　　That presses him from sleep.
LEONTES   What noise there, ho?

Leontes expresses great displeasure at Paulina's arrival with the baby. He orders Antigonus to throw her out of his chamber. Paulina refuses to leave and strongly defends Hermione's honour.

1 How much humour? (in small groups)

Some productions exploit the potential for humour during Paulina's quarrel with Leontes (lines 52–129). For example, one production made the audience laugh frequently by showing everyone, even Leontes, nervous about waking the baby. In a production for which you were responsible decide:
- which moments could be made humorous
- whether you would wish to make them funny or not, and why
- what Shakespeare's purpose might be in providing these opportunities for humour.

2 'By combat make her good ...'

In lines 60–1, Paulina is referring to the old rules of chivalry by which a knight would fight for the reputation of his lady. She is sarcastic about the courage of the lords, implying that even the 'worst' should wish to fight for Hermione's honour. Think of a single word which you think best describes Paulina's tone in lines 60–1. Compare your word with those of other students.

3 Stage direction

[*She lays down the baby*] is one of the stage directions added by editors (see page 34). When Paulina says, 'Here 'tis', what do you think is the most appropriate thing for her to do with the baby? Lay her on the throne? On the floor? Put her in Leontes' arms? In the arms of another lord? Make your own suggestion.

---

needful conference necessary discussion
gossips godparents (at baby's baptism)
Commit imprison
take the rein assume control
liege lord
makes but trifles of doesn't care about
mankind unfeminine
intelligencing bawd! spying go-between, cunning madam

PAULINA No noise, my lord, but needful conference   40
    About some gossips for your highness.
LEONTES   How?
    Away with that audacious lady! Antigonus,
    I charged thee that she should not come about me.
    I knew she would.
ANTIGONUS   I told her so, my lord,
    On your displeasure's peril and on mine,   45
    She should not visit you.
LEONTES   What? Canst not rule her?
PAULINA From all dishonesty he can. In this,
    Unless he take the course that you have done –
    Commit me for committing honour – trust it,
    He shall not rule me.
ANTIGONUS   La you now, you hear!   50
    When she will take the rein, I let her run;
    But she'll not stumble.
PAULINA   Good my liege, I come –
    And I beseech you hear me, who professes
    Myself your loyal servant, your physician,
    Your most obedient counsellor, yet that dares   55
    Less appear so in comforting your evils
    Than such as most seem yours – I say, I come
    From your good queen.
LEONTES   Good queen!
PAULINA Good queen, my lord, good queen, I say good queen,
    And would by combat make her good, so were I   60
    A man, the worst about you.
LEONTES   Force her hence.
PAULINA Let him that makes but trifles of his eyes
    First hand me. On mine own accord I'll off,
    But first I'll do my errand. The good queen –
    For she is good – hath brought you forth a daughter;   65
    Here 'tis; commends it to your blessing.

[She lays down the baby]

LEONTES   Out!
    A mankind witch! Hence with her, out o'door!
    A most intelligencing bawd!

> *Paulina defends herself against Leontes' accusations of dishonesty.*
> *He mocks Antigonus' inability to control her. Paulina says Leontes*
> *wrongfully betrays his family's honour. He delivers a death sentence.*

1 Eye contact (in groups of three)

Take parts as Leontes, Antigonus and Paulina. In lines 75–82 ('Take
up the bastard' – 'Nor I'), Paulina and Leontes have conflicting
objectives. Read the lines through to yourself several times to work out
what you are aiming for. Then, speak the lines. If you are playing the
part of Leontes or Paulina, try to make Antigonus do what you want by
force of eye contact and personality.

2 Paulina's passionate words

Paulina seems to get carried away by the force of her commitment to
Hermione's cause. At lines 80–1 she implies that if Leontes were afraid
of Hermione he would know his child was his. However, perhaps
because of her passionate intensity, the precise meaning of her lines
83–90 is not easy to work out. Speak the lines two or three times, then
try to sum up her meaning in your own words. ('For, as the case now
stands, it is a curse/He cannot be compelled to't', could mean –
because he is the king, it's a shame he cannot be forced to change his
opinion.)

3 'Commit them to the fire!'

This is the second time that Leontes has thought of burning his wife,
and now he wants the child burnt too. Look back at lines 8–9 to remind
yourself of his earlier reason for having Hermione burnt.

ignorant lacking in skill
entitling me calling me by that
 name
dotard old fool
woman-tired hen-pecked
Dame Partlet hen (often used for
 nagging woman)

Unvenerable unworthy
forcèd baseness false description
 of bastard
callet nagging woman
dam mother

PAULINA   Not so.
          I am as ignorant in that as you
          In so entitling me, and no less honest   70
          Than you are mad; which is enough, I'll warrant,
          As this world goes, to pass for honest.
LEONTES   Traitors!
          Will you not push her out? Give her the bastard.
          [*To Antigonus*] Thou dotard, thou art woman-tired, unroosted
          By thy Dame Partlet here. Take up the bastard;   75
          Take't up, I say. Give't to thy crone.
PAULINA   For ever
          Unvenerable be thy hands if thou
          Tak'st up the princess by that forcèd baseness
          Which he has put upon't!
LEONTES   He dreads his wife.
PAULINA So I would you did; then 'twere past all doubt   80
          You'd call your children yours.
LEONTES   A nest of traitors!
ANTIGONUS I am none, by this good light.
PAULINA   Nor I, nor any
          But one that's here, and that's himself; for he
          The sacred honour of himself, his queen's,
          His hopeful son's, his babe's, betrays to slander,   85
          Whose sting is sharper than the sword's; and will not –
          For, as the case now stands, it is a curse
          He cannot be compelled to't – once remove
          The root of his opinion, which is rotten
          As ever oak or stone was sound.
LEONTES   A callet   90
          Of boundless tongue, who late hath beat her husband
          And now baits me! This brat is none of mine;
          It is the issue of Polixenes.
          Hence with it, and together with the dam
          Commit them to the fire!

Paulina describes the baby's likeness to Leontes, who threatens to have Antigonus hanged and Paulina burnt. She continues to defy him, telling him his uncontrolled imagination is to blame. He orders her away.

1 'Behold, my lords' (in small groups)

What do the lords do when Paulina is describing the baby? And what does Paulina do as she speaks? Take parts and explore ways of speaking and reacting to lines 95–107.

2 Colours of emotions (in pairs)

Many cultures use the symbolism of colour for emotion. For example, in Hindu poetry white is associated with joy and blue-black with passion. Shakespeare often associated colours with emotions; for example, red for passion or anger, green for jealousy or envy, white for fear. In line 106, Paulina uses yellow as the colour of suspicion. Talk together about the effectiveness of using colour imagery to express emotions.

3 'Hang all the husbands'

Antigonus wryly comments that if Leontes were to hang all husbands who could not prevent their wives from speaking out, he would have very few subjects left. How might Antigonus say lines 109–11? Would you want him to get a laugh from the audience, or would that be inappropriate at this point in the play?

4 'On your allegiance ...'

In a final attempt to command obedience, Leontes resorts to his royal power. On his coronation all the nobility would have sworn obedience and allegiance to the throne. Invent a suitable gesture for Leontes as he speaks line 120.

---

losel villain
stay her tongue silence her

weak-hinged fancy foolish
  imagination
savours smells

PAULINA   It is yours;   95
    And, might we lay th'old proverb to your charge,
    'So like you, 'tis the worse.' Behold, my lords,
    Although the print be little, the whole matter
    And copy of the father: eye, nose, lip,
    The trick of's frown, his forehead, nay, the valley,   100
    The pretty dimples of his chin and cheek, his smiles,
    The very mould and frame of hand, nail, finger.
    And thou, good goddess Nature, which hast made it
    So like to him that got it, if thou hast
    The ordering of the mind too, 'mongst all colours   105
    No yellow in't, lest she suspect, as he does,
    Her children not her husband's!
LEONTES   A gross hag!
    And, losel, thou art worthy to be hanged,
    That wilt not stay her tongue.
ANTIGONUS   Hang all the husbands
    That cannot do that feat, you'll leave yourself   110
    Hardly one subject.
LEONTES   Once more, take her hence.
PAULINA A most unworthy and unnatural lord
    Can do no more.
LEONTES   I'll ha' thee burnt.
PAULINA   I care not:
    It is an heretic that makes the fire,
    Not she which burns in't. I'll not call you tyrant;   115
    But this most cruel usage of your queen –
    Not able to produce more accusation
    Than your own weak-hinged fancy – something savours
    Of tyranny, and will ignoble make you,
    Yea, scandalous to the world.
LEONTES   On your allegiance,   120
    Out of the chamber with her! Were I a tyrant,
    Where were her life? She durst not call me so
    If she did know me one. Away with her!

Paulina leaves. Leontes calls Antigonus a traitor and tells him to take the baby and have it burnt. The lords kneel and beg Leontes to change his mind. Leontes says he will let the child live.

Identify all the characters in this picture and choose an appropriate line as a caption.

1 'I am a feather'

Why does Leontes relent about burning the baby? Write a paragraph of prose, exploring his thoughts in more detail. You will need to read on to line 182 to see how 'feather'-like, or changeable, Leontes really is.

Jove king of the gods
tender o'er caring about
bastard brains baby's brains

proper own
set'st on encouraged
So to esteem you to acknowledge this
foul issue dreadful result

PAULINA I pray you do not push me, I'll be gone.
        Look to your babe, my lord; 'tis yours. Jove send her   125
        A better guiding spirit! What needs these hands?
        You that are thus so tender o'er his follies
        Will never do him good, not one of you.
        So, so; farewell, we are gone.   *Exit*
LEONTES Thou, traitor, hast set on thy wife to this.   130
        My child? Away with't! Even thou, that hast
        A heart so tender o'er it, take it hence
        And see it instantly consumed with fire;
        Even thou, and none but thou. Take it up straight!
        Within this hour bring me word 'tis done,   135
        And by good testimony, or I'll seize thy life,
        With what thou else call'st thine. If thou refuse,
        And wilt encounter with my wrath, say so;
        The bastard brains with these my proper hands
        Shall I dash out. Go, take it to the fire,   140
        For thou set'st on thy wife.
ANTIGONUS   I did not, sir.
        These lords, my noble fellows, if they please,
        Can clear me in't.
LORDS   We can. My royal liege,
        He is not guilty of her coming hither.
LEONTES You're liars all.   145
LORD Beseech your highness, give us better credit.
        We have always truly served you, and beseech
        So to esteem of us; and on our knees we beg,
        As recompense of our dear services
        Past and to come, that you do change this purpose,   150
        Which being so horrible, so bloody, must
        Lead on to some foul issue. We all kneel.
LEONTES I am a feather for each wind that blows.
        Shall I live on to see this bastard kneel
        And call me father? Better burn it now   155
        Than curse it then. But be it; let it live.

Leontes declares that the baby must die. He orders Antigonus to swear obedience and instructs him to abandon the baby in a foreign land. Antigonus hopes nature will guard the baby.

1 'This female bastard' (in pairs)

In lines 174–82, Leontes refers to the baby as 'it' seven times. Take turns to speak the lines, using different ways of emphasising 'it' (for example, bitterly, or scornfully, and so on). Your task is to express Leontes' feelings as forcefully as possible.

2 Abandoned to Nature

In some cultures, it was an accepted practice to abandon unwanted children: to leave them to the gods and thus to avoid the sin of murder. There are several myths and folk-tales about abandoned babies being found and brought up by animals. In Roman mythology, the twins Romulus and Remus were thrown into the River Tiber. The river stopped and a she-wolf fed them with her milk until a shepherd found and educated them.

Antigonus prays that a spirit will 'instruct the kites and ravens/To be thy nurses!'. 'Wolves and bears ... have done/Like offices of pity.' Imagine that here some lines have been lost from the original script of *The Winter's Tale* after 'pity', line 188. Step into Shakespeare's shoes and write 4 to 6 more lines in the same style as Antigonus using animal imagery (lions, tigers, and so on).

3 'Poor thing, condemned to loss!'

Keep line 191 in mind as you read on. It hints at the name that Hermione gives the baby: Perdita, the lost one (see Act 3 Scene 3, lines 31–3).

Lady Margery hen (nickname)
enjoin command
liegeman subject
commend commit

strangely to some place to some foreign place
Like offices similar duties
In ... require! more than you deserve as a result of doing this

It shall not neither. You, sir, come you hither:
You that have been so tenderly officious
With Lady Margery, your midwife there,
To save this bastard's life – for 'tis a bastard,   160
So sure as this beard's grey – what will you adventure
To save this brat's life?
ANTIGONUS   Anything, my lord,
        That my ability may undergo,
        And nobleness impose. At least thus much –
        I'll pawn the little blood which I have left   165
        To save the innocent. Anything possible.
LEONTES It shall be possible. Swear by this sword
        Thou wilt perform my bidding.
ANTIGONUS   I will, my lord.
LEONTES Mark, and perform it – see'st thou? For the fail
        Of any point in't shall not only be   170
        Death to thyself but to thy lewd-tongued wife,
        Whom for this time we pardon. We enjoin thee,
        As thou art liegeman to us, that thou carry
        This female bastard hence, and that thou bear it
        To some remote and desert place, quite out   175
        Of our dominions; and that there thou leave it,
        Without more mercy, to it own protection
        And favour of the climate. As by strange fortune
        It came to us, I do in justice charge thee,
        On thy soul's peril and thy body's torture,   180
        That thou commend it strangely to some place
        Where chance may nurse or end it. Take it up.
ANTIGONUS I swear to do this, though a present death
        Had been more merciful. Come on, poor babe;
        Some powerful spirit instruct the kites and ravens   185
        To be thy nurses! Wolves and bears, they say,
        Casting their savageness aside, have done
        Like offices of pity. Sir, be prosperous
        In more than this deed does require! And blessing
        Against this cruelty fight on thy side,   190
        Poor thing, condemned to loss!   *Exit [with the baby]*
LEONTES   No, I'll not rear
        Another's issue.

A servant tells Leontes that Cleomenes and Dion have returned from the oracle. Leontes is pleased that they have been so quick and orders a public trial for Hermione.

1 A lord tells his story

Imagine you are one of Leontes' lords who tried to prevent Paulina entering at line 26. You have seen all that followed in Scene 3. Invent a name for yourself and write your diary entry describing your view of events. Include:

- your guess at the reasons for Leontes' behaviour
- the conflict between your feelings about Hermione and the baby, and your sworn loyalty to the king
- your fears about what might happen to Antigonus and the child
- your hopes for the contents of the oracle.

2 Leontes' true intentions? (in pairs)

One person speaks Leontes' lines 197–206 slowly. The other person echoes all the words which suggest that far from giving her a 'just and open trial', Leontes has prejudged Hermione. Then turn back to lines 1–9 and repeat the same echoing activity. Have Leontes' intentions changed in the course of Scene 3?

3 Preparing for the trial (in groups of three)

Improvise a scene in which Emilia and Paulina help Hermione prepare for her appearance in court.

posts messengers
accompt expectation

session court
arraign put on trial

Enter a SERVANT

SERVANT   Please your highness, posts
          From those you sent to th'oracle are come
          An hour since: Cleomenes and Dion,
          Being well arrived from Delphos, are both landed,   195
          Hasting to th'court.
LORD   So please you, sir, their speed
          Hath been beyond accompt.
LEONTES   Twenty-three days
          They have been absent. 'Tis good speed; foretells
          The great Apollo suddenly will have
          The truth of this appear. Prepare you, lords;   200
          Summon a session, that we may arraign
          Our most disloyal lady; for as she hath
          Been publicly accused, so shall she have
          A just and open trial. While she lives
          My heart will be a burden to me. Leave me,   205
          And think upon my bidding.

                                                    Exeunt

Looking back at Act 2
Activities for groups or individuals

1 Male *versus* female

Act 2 opens with a gentle domestic scene invaded by male authority. One effect that this can have in performance is to suggest to the audience Hermione's lack of power. Work out how you might stage the opening, and how far you would emphasise this male dominance in a production for which you were responsible.

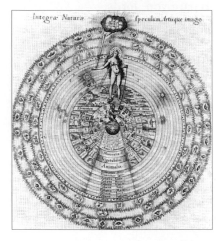

'There's some ill planet reigns' (Scene 1, line 105). This 1617 drawing of the Universe is based on Ptolemy's theory that the earth was at the centre. Many people believed that disastrous events on earth were caused by the influence of planets (see Activity 2 on page 42).

2 Hermione's prison

Queen Hermione is sent to prison by her jealous husband. When Shakespeare was writing there were different grades of prison for different classes of prisoner. Even in prison social status was preserved. High-ranking persons were incarcerated in castles, or places like the Tower of London. Ordinary criminals were fortunate if they were sent to prison. For them, a more common punishment was mutilation. The future Queen Elizabeth was virtually imprisoned during the reign of her sister, Mary. After Elizabeth became Queen, she imprisoned Mary Queen of Scots.

Scene 2 is the only 'prison scene' in the play, and most modern productions try to portray the prison symbolically, without an elaborate set. Design your own set for Scene 2.

3 Not guilty?

Paulina claims that the baby born to Hermione was 'Freed and enfranchised' by 'great nature'. Organise a debate on the proposition: 'This house believes that children are born without sin.'

4 'Purge him of that humour'

Paulina considers that Leontes must be mentally sick to behave as he does. She hopes to cleanse ('purge') him with her news of the baby.

Paulina's words echo a popular belief in Shakespeare's time, which claimed that there were four fluids (humours) in the body. For perfect physical and mental health all the so-called cardinal humours had to be in proportion.

FLUID/HUMOUR	TEMPERAMENT	ATTRIBUTE
blood	sanguine	bravery
phlegm	phlegmatic	calmness
black bile	melancholic	melancholy
yellowe	choleric	anger

Illnesses could be caused by an imbalance in the humours, and Leontes has an excess of one humour (which?).

Do you think that this theory of 'humours' has any validity today? For example, does it apply in any way to your temperament?

5 Husband and wife

What kind of marriage do Antigonus and Paulina have?

a Improvise two scenes between them: one where he does seem to be hen-pecked by his wife, and one where they are on an equal footing, and he respects her judgement. Find justification in the script for both readings. Decide which presentation you think is more truthful.

b 'He shall not rule me' says Paulina (Scene 3, line 50). Over the years several instruction books have been written, detailing the correct behaviour for wives. Write your own modern version, giving your ideas about appropriate behaviour for a wife (or husband). Begin by identifying three or four rules that Leontes probably has in mind for *his* wife.

*Returning from Delphi, Cleomenes and Dion discuss the beauty of the
island and the people. They recall the impact on them of the oracle
ceremony and hope their journey will prove favourable for Hermione.*

1 Consulting the oracle

In line 2, Cleomenes speaks of the 'isle', but Delphi is on the Greek
mainland. Perhaps Shakespeare was thinking of Delos, in classical
mythology the island of Apollo. Traditionally, Apollo's temple at
Delphi was revered as a place where the future could be foretold.

The priestess at Delphi was always called Pythia. She sat on a three-
legged stool and inhaled the sulphurous vapour from deep within the
earth. Her eyes sparkled, her hair stood on end and shivering ran over
all her naked body. In 1997, it was discovered that the vapour is
hallucinogenic.

The priest took down the oracle's inspired words. These were
originally spoken in hexameter verse (12-syllable lines), but when some
Greeks pointed out that Apollo, god of poetry, produced appalling
verse, later oracles were delivered in prose. The oracle was usually
consulted in spring.

Before you read on, make a note of what you think will be in the
sealed message from the oracle, and what Leontes' reaction will be.

2 Visiting the shrine (in small groups)

A film version of *The Winter's Tale* is being considered. You have been
commissioned to write a screenplay for the visit to Apollo's shrine using
all the information given in Scene 1. Remember to work carefully on
establishing an appropriately reverent atmosphere. You should include
some of the following: locations, costumes, ritual, offerings, camera
angles, sound and lighting effects.

---

celestial habits heavenly robes
event outcome, result
is worth the use on't has been
  well spent

carriage conducting
great divine principal priest
discover reveal

ACT 3   SCENE 1
Sicilia: near the sea coast

Enter CLEOMENES *and* DION

CLEOMENES The climate's delicate, the air most sweet,
    Fertile the isle, the temple much surpassing
    The common praise it bears.
DION   I shall report,
    For most it caught me, the celestial habits
    (Methinks I so should term them) and the reverence   5
    Of the grave wearers. O, the sacrifice!
    How ceremonious, solemn, and unearthly
    It was i'th'off'ring!
CLEOMENES   But of all, the burst
    And the ear-deaf'ning voice o'th'oracle,
    Kin to Jove's thunder, so surprised my sense   10
    That I was nothing.
DION   If th'event o'th'journey
    Prove as successful to the queen – O be't so! –
    As it hath been to us rare, pleasant, speedy,
    The time is worth the use on't.
CLEOMENES   Great Apollo
    Turn all to th'best! These proclamations,   15
    So forcing faults upon Hermione,
    I little like.
DION   The violent carriage of it
    Will clear or end the business, when the oracle
    (Thus by Apollo's great divine sealed up)
    Shall the contents discover. Something rare   20
    Even then will rush to knowledge. Go; fresh horses,
    And gracious be the issue!

                 Exeunt

Leontes declares he is no tyrant because Hermione is to be tried in open court. The officer reads the charge of treason, accusing Hermione of committing adultery and plotting to kill Leontes.

1 Hiding behind his status (in pairs)

One person speaks Leontes' lines 1–7. The other person then speaks the speech using the singular personal pronoun (I, me, my) where Leontes uses the royal plural (we, us, our). Talk together about the different effects produced. Which version has more emotional impact on you?

2 Staging the trial (in small groups)

This is a public trial which later Hermione says is 'i'th'open air' (line 103). Some productions ignore her words and set the scene inside a courtroom. Discuss how you would stage it.

3 The Officer's tone?

Would you wish to have the audience understand what the Officer's opinion of the trial might be? For example, how does he say 'partly laid open' (line 17)?

4 Hermione's costume

How should Hermione be dressed when she is brought into the court? She has recently borne a child and has come from prison, so might be in a plain robe. One production portrayed her barefoot and in sackcloth. Another brought her on in the full majesty of her coronation robes. Sketch a design for Hermione's costume.

Even pushes 'gainst our heart
  strikes even to my heart
purgation acquittal

indictment charge
pretence plot

ACT 3   SCENE 2
Sicilia: a court of justice

Enter LEONTES, LORDS, *and* OFFICERS

LEONTES This sessions, to our great grief we pronounce,
　　　　Even pushes 'gainst our heart: the party tried
　　　　The daughter of a king, our wife, and one
　　　　Of us too much beloved. Let us be cleared
　　　　Of being tyrannous, since we so openly　　　　　　　　5
　　　　Proceed in justice, which shall have due course,
　　　　Even to the guilt or the purgation.
　　　　Produce the prisoner.
OFFICER It is his highness' pleasure that the queen
　　　　Appear in person here in court.　　　　　　　　　　10

Enter HERMIONE, *as to her trial,* [PAULINA, *and*] LADIES

　　　　　　　　　　　　　Silence!
LEONTES Read the indictment.
OFFICER　　[*Reads*] Hermione, queen to the worthy Leontes, King of
　Sicilia, thou art here accused and arraigned of high treason, in
　committing adultery with Polixenes, King of Bohemia, and con-
　spiring with Camillo to take away the life of our sovereign lord the　　15
　king, thy royal husband; the pretence whereof being by circum-
　stances partly laid open, thou, Hermione, contrary to the faith and
　allegiance of a true subject, didst counsel and aid them, for their
　better safety, to fly away by night.

Hermione speaks in her own defence, arguing that she is innocent of the charge brought against her. Leontes says that all those who are corrupt enough to commit a crime are corrupt enough to deny it.

1 The speech for the defence (in small groups)

An actor who played Hermione said,

> 'Her speech has a fluidity and simplicity compared to the more complex intellectual agility of the first scene, where she played with words. She is articulate, objective and strong, because she is right. She is innocent and she knows it. She does not have to plead her cause or prove that she is true. She has faith.'

Breaking the speech down into manageable sense units can help the actor's understanding and delivery. Use the sense units below to suggest what advice you would give the actor about how to maintain the audience's attention as she speaks.

Lines 20–6	I feel it is pointless to say I am innocent. My honesty is called dishonesty.
Lines 26–30	The gods are watching and will see justice done.
Lines 30–5	You know, Leontes, my past behaviour was as truly innocent as my present unhappiness is without parallel.
Lines 35–40	I, a queen and the mother of the prince, must now plead in public for my life and honour.
Lines 40–3	I am not begging for my life, but my honour must be preserved for Mamillius' sake.
Lines 43–52	I appeal to you. Remember how I have always behaved and believe that nothing dishonourable has occurred. If one thing can be proved against me, let everyone here condemn me.

---

boot me do me any good
powers divine the gods
continent innocent, faithful
pattern give an example of
owe/A moiety own a half share
hopeful promising
prate plead to no purpose

for honour, ... I stand for my honour is what I bequeath to my children and that is all I am fighting for
uncurrent devalued or debased
bound limits
gainsay deny

HERMIONE   Since what I am to say must be but that   20
                Which contradicts my accusation, and
                The testimony on my part no other
                But what comes from myself, it shall scarce boot me
                To say 'Not guilty'. Mine integrity,
                Being counted falsehood, shall, as I express it,   25
                Be so received. But thus: if powers divine
                Behold our human actions, as they do,
                I doubt not then but innocence shall make
                False accusation blush, and tyranny
                Tremble at patience. You, my lord, best know –   30
                Who least will seem to do so – my past life
                Hath been as continent, as chaste, as true,
                As I am now unhappy; which is more
                Than history can pattern, though devised
                And played to take spectators. For behold me,   35
                A fellow of the royal bed, which owe
                A moiety of the throne, a great king's daughter,
                The mother to a hopeful prince, here standing
                To prate and talk for life and honour 'fore
                Who please to come and hear. For life, I prize it   40
                As I weigh grief, which I would spare; for honour,
                'Tis a derivative from me to mine,
                And only that I stand for. I appeal
                To your own conscience, sir, before Polixenes
                Came to your court, how I was in your grace,   45
                How merited to be so; since he came,
                With what encounter so uncurrent I
                Have strained t'appear thus: if one jot beyond
                The bound of honour, or in act or will
                That way inclining, hardened be the hearts   50
                Of all that hear me, and my near'st of kin
                Cry fie upon my grave!
LEONTES   I ne'er heard yet
                That any of these bolder vices wanted
                Less impudence to gainsay what they did
                Than to perform it first.

Hermione says that she loved Polixenes only as much as Leontes had commanded and knows nothing of conspiracy or of Camillo's departure. Leontes will not believe her and threatens her with death.

'Your actions are my dreams.' Leontes' dream is a nightmare which recalls the visual nature of his earlier imaginings about Hermione and Polixenes. How would you stage this moment in the play?

due applicable	**Those of your fact** those proved
Wotting knowing	to be adulterers as you are
undertane promised	**concerns more than avails** is not
in the level range, as the target	worth the trouble

HERMIONE   That's true enough,   55
    Though 'tis a saying, sir, not due to me.
LEONTES   You will not own it.
HERMIONE   More than mistress of
    Which comes to me in name of fault, I must not
    At all acknowledge. For Polixenes,
    With whom I am accused, I do confess   60
    I loved him as in honour he required:
    With such a kind of love as might become
    A lady like me, with a love even such,
    So and no other, as yourself commanded;
    Which not to have done I think had been in me   65
    Both disobedience and ingratitude
    To you, and toward your friend, whose love had spoke
    Even since it could speak, from an infant, freely
    That it was yours. Now, for conspiracy,
    I know not how it tastes, though it be dished   70
    For me to try how. All I know of it
    Is that Camillo was an honest man;
    And why he left your court the gods themselves,
    Wotting no more than I, are ignorant.
LEONTES You knew of his departure, as you know   75
    What you have undertane to do in's absence.
HERMIONE Sir,
    You speak a language that I understand not.
    My life stands in the level of your dreams,
    Which I'll lay down.
LEONTES   Your actions are my dreams.   80
    You had a bastard by Polixenes,
    And I but dreamed it. As you were past all shame –
    Those of your fact are so – so past all truth,
    Which to deny concerns more than avails; for as
    Thy brat hath been cast out, like to itself,   85
    No father owning it – which is indeed
    More criminal in thee than it – so thou
    Shalt feel our justice, in whose easiest passage
    Look for no less than death.

Hermione says that she is not afraid to die because everything she values in life has been taken from her. But for her honour's sake she demands that the oracle be read.

1 'Apollo be my judge!'

Hermione says that she is not afraid to die. She lists the many terrible things that have already happened to her. She has lost Leontes' love – 'the crown and comfort' of her life; she is not allowed to see her son; her baby has been taken from her to be killed; she is publicly proclaimed a whore; she has not been allowed time to recover after childbirth but rushed to this open-air trial. Her honour is all that has she left to value. She warns Leontes that if he condemns her on suspicion alone it will be tyranny and not justice. She asks the court to hear the oracle and declares that she will accept the judgement of Apollo.

As she awaits the oracle she wishes that her father, the Emperor of Russia, was present watching her trial, to pity the depth of her wretchedness, but not to seek revenge.

a Use the summary above to help you speak Hermione's lines.

b What is Leontes doing during Hermione's speeches? Listening intently? Showing guilt? Talking to courtiers, trying to ignore Hermione? Advise the actor.

c What do the lords do as Hermione speaks? Step into role as a lord and suggest how you would behave throughout her two speeches. Remember, whatever you do must help the audience to understand Hermione's language.

bug monster
commodity advantage
Starred most unluckily born under a very unlucky star
Haled dragged
post public notice
child-bed privilege period of rest after childbirth
all fashion every class
strength of limit time to recover my strength
surmises speculations
rigour tyranny
flatness depth

HERMIONE   Sir, spare your threats.
  The bug which you would fright me with, I seek.   90
  To me can life be no commodity:
  The crown and comfort of my life, your favour,
  I do give lost, for I do feel it gone,
  But know not how it went. My second joy,
  And first-fruits of my body, from his presence   95
  I am barred like one infectious. My third comfort,
  Starred most unluckily, is from my breast –
  The innocent milk in it most innocent mouth –
  Haled out to murder. Myself on every post
  Proclaimed a strumpet; with immodest hatred   100
  The child-bed privilege denied, which 'longs
  To women of all fashion; lastly, hurried
  Here to this place, i'th'open air, before
  I have got strength of limit. Now, my liege,
  Tell me what blessings I have here alive   105
  That I should fear to die. Therefore proceed.
  But yet hear this – mistake me not: no life,
  I prize it not a straw, but for mine honour,
  Which I would free – if I shall be condemned
  Upon surmises, all proofs sleeping else   110
  But what your jealousies awake, I tell you
  'Tis rigour and not law. Your honours all,
  I do refer me to the oracle:
  Apollo be my judge!
LORD   This your request
  Is altogether just. Therefore bring forth,   115
  And in Apollo's name, his oracle.

        [*Exeunt certain Officers*]

HERMIONE The Emperor of Russia was my father.
  O that he were alive, and here beholding
  His daughter's trial! That he did but see
  The flatness of my misery; yet with eyes   120
  Of pity, not revenge!

The oracle is unsealed. Though it declares the innocence of Hermione,
Leontes does not believe it. A servant reports the death of Mamillius.
Hermione faints.

1 High drama (in large groups)

The lines opposite make an intensely dramatic episode in the performance. In many productions the opening of the oracle is performed with great ceremony, like a formal religious ritual. Such dignity contrasts starkly with the action that follows, as Leontes vehemently rejects the oracle's message, hears of the death of his son, and sees the apparent death of his wife.

Stage the lines opposite, using the following points to help your preparations.

- Invent a ceremony for lines 122–33.
- What will your 'sealed-up oracle' look like? One production used a pottery vessel which was smashed open.
- Identify each distinct action that takes place.
- How can you use non-speaking characters to increase dramatic effect (for example, lords, ladies, officers)?
- Identify the different atmospheres you can create as the episode proceeds. (You will find that Shakespeare provides language that enables the actors to change the prevailing mood very quickly.)
- Try to tell the story on the opposite page through mimed action.
- Much of the oracle's message (lines 130–3) is perfectly clear, but the final part ('and the king ... found') is enigmatic. How do the listeners react to each separate part of the oracle's verdict?

sessions trial
conceit thinking about
speed fate

[*Enter* OFFICERS, *with* CLEOMENES *and* DION]

OFFICER   You here shall swear upon this sword of justice
That, you, Cleomenes and Dion, have
Been both at Delphos, and from thence have brought
This sealed-up oracle, by the hand delivered   125
Of great Apollo's priest; and that since then
You have not dared to break the holy seal,
Nor read the secrets in't.
CLEOMENES *and* DION   All this we swear.
LEONTES   Break up the seals, and read.
OFFICER   [*Reads*] Hermione is chaste, Polixenes blameless, Camillo a   130
   true subject, Leontes a jealous tyrant, his innocent babe truly
   begotten, and the king shall live without an heir, if that which is
   lost be not found.
LORDS   Now blessèd be the great Apollo!
HERMIONE   Praised!
LEONTES   Hast thou read truth?
OFFICER   Ay, my lord, even so   135
As it is here set down.
LEONTES   There is no truth at all i'th'oracle!
The sessions shall proceed: this is mere falsehood.

[*Enter a* SERVANT]

SERVANT   My lord the king, the king!
LEONTES   What is the business?
SERVANT   O sir, I shall be hated to report it!   140
The prince your son, with mere conceit and fear
Of the queen's speed, is gone.
LEONTES   How! Gone?
SERVANT   Is dead.
LEONTES   Apollo's angry, and the heavens themselves
Do strike at my injustice.
                          [*Hermione faints*]
                             How now there!
PAULINA   This news is mortal to the queen. Look down   145
And see what death is doing.

Leontes directs the ladies to revive Hermione. He asks Apollo for forgiveness for doubting the honesty of Hermione, Camillo and Polixenes. Paulina re-enters in deep sorrow.

1 Sincere repentance? (in pairs)

Just as Leontes' jealousy possessed him instantly and irrationally, his repentance is equally abrupt. Share out a delivery of Leontes' lines, with each person speaking a short section (a 'sense unit') in turn.

Afterwards, decide what you think about the swiftness of Leontes' conversion. Do you think it is heartfelt or superficial?

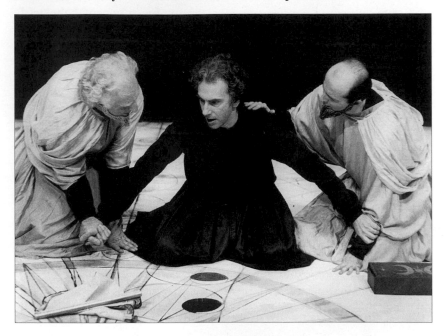

'Apollo, pardon';
Leontes begs forgiveness for disbelieving the oracle.

---

o'ercharged under stress
profaneness blasphemy
transported carried away
tardied delayed
Unclasped revealed
practice plot

commended committed
No richer than his honour
  having no fortune apart from
  his honour
my lace the fastening of my corset

LEONTES   Take her hence.
Her heart is but o'ercharged; she will recover.
I have too much believed mine own suspicion.
Beseech you, tenderly apply to her
Some remedies for life.

        [Exeunt Paulina and Ladies, with Hermione]

                    Apollo, pardon   150
My great profaneness 'gainst thine oracle.
I'll reconcile me to Polixenes,
New woo my queen, recall the good Camillo,
Whom I proclaim a man of truth, of mercy:
For, being transported by my jealousies   155
To bloody thoughts and to revenge, I chose
Camillo for the minister to poison
My friend Polixenes; which had been done,
But that the good mind of Camillo tardied
My swift command, though I with death and with   160
Reward did threaten and encourage him,
Not doing it and being done. He, most humane
And filled with honour, to my kingly guest
Unclasped my practice, quit his fortunes here –
Which you knew great – and to the hazard   165
Of all incertainties himself commended,
No richer than his honour. How he glisters
Thorough my rust! And how his piety
Does my deeds make the blacker!

             [Enter PAULINA*]*

PAULINA   Woe the while!
O cut my lace, lest my heart, cracking it,   170
Break too!
LORD   What fit is this, good lady?

Paulina calls Leontes a tyrant and asks what punishment he has in store for her. She lists all his wicked actions, but says they are nothing compared with his final tyranny: causing Hermione's death.

1 Advice to actors

Paulina's speech divides into several units leading to a dreadful climax. She asks Leontes how he is going to torture her, speaks of his tyranny, and of his betrayal of both Polixenes and Camillo. She reminds him of his rejection of his new-born daughter and the death of his young son. All these, she says, are nothing compared with his responsibility for Hermione's death.

a Suggest how Paulina should deliver each section of her speech.

b What should Leontes do during Paulina's speech? For example, decide whether Leontes is completely cowed or tries to interrupt Paulina.

c How many courtiers should be on stage? Might some of Hermione's women return with Paulina? Work out how these non-speaking actors might behave.

d Choose a moment in Paulina's speech and draw a stage plan indicating who is there and where they are placed to create the most effective stage grouping.

2 Instruments of torture

The professional torturer was horribly inventive when it came to devising methods of inflicting pain. Wheels and racks (line 173) were used to break the limbs of victims. To flay someone was to skin them alive. Suggest one or two reasons why Paulina uses such cruel images.

---

studied well planned
Fancies fantasies
but spices merely a taste
or none or little smallest of crimes
shed water out of fire wept in
  hell
high noble

tender young
conceive believe
dam mother
Laid to thy answer set down as
  accusation against you
dropped down come down from
  heaven

PAULINA What studied torments, tyrant, hast for me?
         What wheels, racks, fires? What flaying, boiling
         In leads or oils? What old or newer torture
         Must I receive, whose every word deserves   175
         To taste of thy most worst? Thy tyranny,
         Together working with thy jealousies –
         Fancies too weak for boys, too green and idle
         For girls of nine – O think what they have done,
         And then run mad indeed, stark mad, for all   180
         Thy bygone fooleries were but spices of it.
         That thou betrayedst Polixenes 'twas nothing:
         That did but show thee of a fool, inconstant,
         And damnable ingrateful. Nor was't much
         Thou wouldst have poisoned good Camillo's honour   185
         To have him kill a king – poor trespasses,
         More monstrous standing by; whereof I reckon
         The casting forth to crows thy baby daughter
         To be or none or little, though a devil
         Would have shed water out of fire ere done't.   190
         Nor is't directly laid to thee, the death
         Of the young prince, whose honourable thoughts –
         Thoughts high for one so tender – cleft the heart
         That could conceive a gross and foolish sire
         Blemished his gracious dam. This is not, no,   195
         Laid to thy answer. But the last – O lords,
         When I have said, cry woe! The queen, the queen,
         The sweet'st, dear'st creature's dead; and vengeance for't
         Not dropped down yet!
LORD   The higher powers forbid!

Paulina repeats that Hermione is dead and wishes Leontes to suffer for all eternity. When a courtier rebukes her, she apologises, acknowledges Leontes' repentance, and wishes for forgiveness.

1 From cursing to comforting (in groups of 8–10)

Paulina's first speech instructs Leontes to despair that Hermione is dead. In her second speech she seems to feel that she has attacked him too strongly. Like Leontes, she too has a very abrupt change of heart, shifting from cursing him with perpetual misery to acknowledging his 'noble heart'.

a One person takes the role of Leontes and stands in the centre of the group. A second person speaks Paulina's first speech (lines 200–11). The rest of the group repeats as a loud echo all of her words which would be especially wounding to Leontes, circling him as they do so. Leontes reacts to each echo (he may eventually end up on the floor in misery). Repeat the exercise, but this time whisper the echo of the wounding words. Which method do you find more dramatically effective?

b In some productions Paulina speaks her second speech extremely sarcastically, suggesting that she does not feel 'He is touched/To th'noble heart.' Try this way of speaking lines 215–29. Talk together about whether you find this an appropriate interpretation.

c Which of Paulina's speeches do you think would be more disturbing to Leontes: the first when she is railing at him, or the second when she seems to be trying to comfort him?

Prevail not do not convince you
Tincture or lustre colour or shine
still continual
that way thou wert towards you
 (in forgiveness)

minded reminded
Take your patience to you suffer
 patiently

PAULINA I say she's dead; I'll swear't. If word nor oath   200
Prevail not, go and see. If you can bring
Tincture or lustre in her lip, her eye,
Heat outwardly or breath within, I'll serve you
As I would do the gods. But O thou tyrant,
Do not repent these things, for they are heavier   205
Than all thy woes can stir. Therefore betake thee
To nothing but despair. A thousand knees,
Ten thousand years together, naked, fasting,
Upon a barren mountain, and still winter
In storm perpetual, could not move the gods   210
To look that way thou wert.

LEONTES   Go on, go on.
Thou canst not speak too much; I have deserved
All tongues to talk their bitt'rest.

LORD   Say no more.
Howe'er the business goes, you have made fault
I'th'boldness of your speech.

PAULINA   I am sorry for't.   215
All faults I make, when I shall come to know them,
I do repent. Alas, I have showed too much
The rashness of a woman! He is touched
To th'noble heart. What's gone and what's past help
Should be past grief. Do not receive affliction   220
At my petition; I beseech you rather
Let me be punished, that have minded you
Of what you should forget. Now, good my liege,
Sir, royal sir, forgive a foolish woman.
The love I bore your queen – lo, fool again!   225
I'll speak of her no more, nor of your children;
I'll not remember you of my own lord,
Who is lost too. Take your patience to you,
And I'll say nothing.

Leontes vows to mourn his wife and son for ever. In Scene 3, Antigonus and a sailor land in Bohemia with Hermione's baby. The sailor fears the rough weather and the anger of the gods.

1 Mourning duties

Leontes says that he will bury Hermione and Mamillius in one grave, and write on the tombstone that he caused their deaths.

a Write the obituaries of Hermione and Mamillius for Sicilia's national newspaper. What will you say about Leontes' role in their deaths?

b Design the tomb. What would be written on it?

2 'Come, and lead me to/These sorrows'

Decide how you would have the cast leave the stage on Leontes' 'Come, and lead me/To these sorrows.'

3 From Sicilia to Bohemia (in small groups)

A quick scene change is required between Scenes 2 and 3 as the action shifts from Sicilia to Bohemia. How might you achieve this? For example, consider how you could indicate to an audience the difference between Sicilia and Bohemia through colour, symbols, lighting, or other effects.

4 'The skies look grimly'

During Scene 3 a thunderstorm increases gradually. When you have read through lines 1–65, decide how you would use sound and lighting effects to create atmosphere. You will find that the mood changes as the storm wanes during the Shepherd's speech. During which lines would you have the climax of the storm? Remember the actors need to be heard and seen too.

---

but well/When most the truth best when telling the complete truth
recreation pastime and re-creation
bear up with give me strength to do

perfect quite sure
deserts deserted areas
have in hand are undertaking
bark ship
keep upon't live here

LEONTES	Thou didst speak but well

When most the truth, which I receive much better   230
Than to be pitied of thee. Prithee, bring me
To the dead bodies of my queen and son.
One grave shall be for both; upon them shall
The causes of their death appear, unto
Our shame perpetual. Once a day I'll visit   235
The chapel where they lie, and tears shed there
Shall be my recreation. So long as nature
Will bear up with this exercise, so long
I daily vow to use it. Come, and lead me
To these sorrows.   240

Exeunt

ACT 3   SCENE 3
Bohemia: the sea coast

Enter ANTIGONUS with the baby, and a MARINER

ANTIGONUS Thou art perfect then our ship hath touched upon
The deserts of Bohemia?

MARINER   Ay, my lord, and fear
We have landed in ill time. The skies look grimly
And threaten present blusters. In my conscience,
The heavens with that we have in hand are angry   5
And frown upon's.

ANTIGONUS Their sacred wills be done! Go, get aboard;
Look to thy bark. I'll not be long before
I call upon thee.

MARINER   Make your best haste, and go not
Too far i'th'land; 'tis like to be loud weather.   10
Besides, this place is famous for the creatures
Of prey that keep upon't.

ANTIGONUS   Go thou away;
I'll follow instantly.

MARINER   I am glad at heart
To be so rid o'th'business.   *Exit*

Antigonus tells of his dream of Hermione. She told him to abandon the child in Bohemia and to name it Perdita, and that he would never see his wife again. He obeys her commands.

1 Antigonus' dream (in small groups)

Antigonus tells the baby about a vivid dream he has had, in which Hermione appeared to him in billowing robes like a ship in full sail ('So filled and so becoming'). She told him to leave the child in Bohemia and to call it Perdita (meaning 'lost'). For his service to Leontes in abandoning the baby, he will never see his wife again. He says he usually does not believe in dreams but for once he does.

Antigonus thinks that the dream means that Hermione has died and that Apollo wishes the child to be abandoned in Bohemia to whatever fate befalls it, because it is truly the child of Polixenes.

How might Antigonus deliver the speech to convey all the key facts clearly to the audience? Work out how Antigonus should manage the baby, the box and the papers, and then present Antigonus' report of his dream as imaginatively as you can, using sound and lighting effects if you have them. You might want to have lines 26–35 spoken by Hermione.

2 'Dreams are toys' (in small groups)

Share your experiences of dreams. Do you agree with Antigonus' opinion that dreams are 'toys' (trivial), or do you think that dreams give you important insights into your life?

3 '*A box and papers*'

What do the box and papers (stage direction, line 45) that Antigonus places beside the baby look like ? When you have read the remainder of the scene, design these two props.

---

very sanctity the epitome of saintliness
anon immediately, then
ungentle business vile task
squared ruled

thy character a written account of you
these (line 46) (see line 107, page 97)
breed thee secure your upbringing
still rest thine always be yours

ANTIGONUS   Come, poor babe.
    I have heard, but not believed, the spirits o'th'dead   15
    May walk again. If such thing be, thy mother
    Appeared to me last night; for ne'er was dream
    So like a waking. To me comes a creature,
    Sometimes her head on one side, some another –
    I never saw a vessel of like sorrow,   20
    So filled and so becoming. In pure white robes,
    Like very sanctity, she did approach
    My cabin where I lay; thrice bowed before me,
    And, gasping to begin some speech, her eyes
    Became two spouts; the fury spent, anon   25
    Did this break from her: 'Good Antigonus,
    Since fate, against thy better disposition,
    Hath made thy person for the thrower-out
    Of my poor babe, according to thine oath,
    Places remote enough are in Bohemia;   30
    There weep, and leave it crying; and for the babe
    Is counted lost for ever, Perdita
    I prithee call't. For this ungentle business
    Put on thee by my lord, thou ne'er shalt see
    Thy wife Paulina more.' And so, with shrieks,   35
    She melted into air. Affrighted much,
    I did in time collect myself, and thought
    This was so, and no slumber. Dreams are toys;
    Yet for this once, yea superstitiously,
    I will be squared by this. I do believe   40
    Hermione hath suffered death, and that
    Apollo would, this being indeed the issue
    Of King Polixenes, it should here be laid,
    Either for life or death, upon the earth
    Of its right father. Blossom, speed thee well!   45

[He lays down the baby, and places a box and papers beside it]

    There lie, and there thy character; there these,
    Which may, if fortune please, both breed thee, pretty,
    And still rest thine.

The storm increases and Antigonus is chased off by a bear.
An old Shepherd enters complaining about the behaviour of young men.
He finds the baby. His son says he has seen strange sights.

1 *'Exit, pursued by a bear'* (in pairs)

This famous stage direction offers rich dramatic opportunities for any director. For example, different productions have presented:

- an actor in a bear's costume
- storm, lightning, sound effects, growling – but no bear
- a model of a bear casting an enormous shadow
- a small actor dressed as a teddy bear, accompanied by the tune of 'The Teddy Bears' Picnic'
- Leontes wearing a large glove like a bear's paw with which he strikes Antigonus
- a 6-metre model of a bear.

a Why do you think Shakespeare introduces a bear?

b Talk together about the directors' possible aims for each of the ideas above.

c Make your own suggestions, and justify them in terms of your ideas about the play. Then use whatever resources you can lay your hands on, and improvise some of your ideas.

2 Lads! – and ladies (in pairs)

In lines 58–62, the Shepherd expresses his low opinion of young men, all of whom misbehave. In lines 69–71, he speculates that the baby is the unwanted result of the liaison of a lady-in-waiting ('some trunk-work, some behind-door-work'). Discuss whether you think the Shepherd is right in his view of young men, and why Shakespeare makes him guess wrongly about the baby's parentage.

---

wronging the ancientry upsetting the old folk
an't be thy will if God wills it
barne bairn, child
scape escapade
stair-work secret love-making

got conceived (begot)
hallowed shouted
talk on gossip over
firmament sky, heavens
bodkin large needle

[*Thunder*]
The storm begins. Poor wretch,
That for thy mother's fault art thus exposed
To loss, and what may follow! Weep I cannot,   50
But my heart bleeds; and most accursed am I
To be by oath enjoined to this. Farewell!
The day frowns more and more; thou'rt like to have
A lullaby too rough. I never saw
The heavens so dim by day. A savage clamour!   55
Well may I get aboard. This is the chase!
I am gone for ever!   *Exit, pursued by a bear*

[*Enter a* SHEPHERD]

SHEPHERD I would there were no age between ten and three-and-twenty,
or that youth would sleep out the rest, for there is nothing in the
between but getting wenches with child, wronging the ancientry,   60
stealing, fighting. Hark you now: would any but these boiled-brains
of nineteen and two-and-twenty hunt this weather? They have
scared away two of my best sheep, which I fear the wolf will
sooner find than the master. If anywhere I have them, 'tis by the
sea-side, browsing of ivy.   65

[*He sees the baby*]

Good luck, an't be thy will, what have we here? Mercy on's, a
barne! A very pretty barne. A boy or a child, I wonder? A pretty
one, a very pretty one. Sure, some scape. Though I am not bookish,
yet I can read waiting-gentlewoman in the scape. This has been
some stair-work, some trunk-work, some behind-door-work. They   70
were warmer that got this than the poor thing is here. I'll take it up
for pity – yet I'll tarry till my son come. He hallowed but even now.
Whoa-ho-hoa!

Enter CLOWN

CLOWN Hilloa, loa!
SHEPHERD What, art so near? If thou'lt see a thing to talk on when thou   75
art dead and rotten, come hither. What ail'st thou, man?
CLOWN I have seen two such sights, by sea and by land! But I am not
to say it is a sea, for it is now the sky; betwixt the firmament and
it you cannot thrust a bodkin's point.

The Shepherd's son describes the storm which sank the ship, drowning all the sailors, and how Antigonus was killed by the bear. The Shepherd shows the baby, and a box which contains gold.

1 Jumbled-up stories

The Shepherd's son is so keen to tell what he has seen that he jumbles up his account of the storm with the report of Antigonus being eaten by the bear. Imagine you are a newspaper reporter. Untangle the events and write your report.

2 Sea change: from death to life

Lines 100–1, 'Thou met'st with things dying, I with things new born.' are often interpreted as the turning point in the play, expressing the idea of death followed by birth. They mark the shift from Sicilia to Bohemia, from court to country, from the abandonment of the child to her adoption, and from tragedy to comedy.

Write a story or a poem using these lines as the theme (see also page 99).

3 The Clown

You have been cast in the role of the Clown, the Shepherd's son. A clown in Shakespeare's plays was not a circus performer but a comic character who provided humour. Consider how you might play the part. Begin by speaking his lines to bring out the muddle and the humour. You could research other Shakespearean clowns, for example, Lavatch in *All's Well That Ends Well*.

4 Open the box! (in pairs)

Lines 105–6 offer wonderful opportunities to comic actors. Work out your own staging of the opening of the box.

---

takes up swallows
yest foam
hogshead barrel of beer
for the land-service what happened on the land
flap-dragoned it swallowed it
lacked footing been useless

bearing-cloth christening wrap
changeling fairy child exchanged for human child
close secret
still permanently
next way quickest route
Marry by the Virgin Mary

SHEPHERD Why, boy, how is it?   80

CLOWN I would you did but see how it chafes, how it rages, how it takes
    up the shore! But that's not to the point. O, the most piteous cry of
    the poor souls! Sometimes to see 'em, and not to see 'em; now the
    ship boring the moon with her main-mast, and anon swallowed
    with yest and froth, as you'd thrust a cork into a hogshead. And   85
    then for the land-service, to see how the bear tore out his
    shoulder-bone, how he cried to me for help and said his name was
    Antigonus, a nobleman! But to make an end of the ship, to see how
    the sea flap-dragoned it; but first, how the poor souls roared, and
    the sea mocked them; and how the poor gentleman roared, and the   90
    bear mocked him, both roaring louder than the sea or weather.

SHEPHERD Name of mercy, when was this, boy?

CLOWN Now, now! I have not winked since I saw these sights. The
    men are not yet cold under water, nor the bear half dined on the
    gentleman: he's at it now.   95

SHEPHERD Would I had been by to have helped the old man!

CLOWN I would you had been by the ship side, to have helped her;
    there your charity would have lacked footing!

SHEPHERD Heavy matters, heavy matters! But look thee here, boy.
    Now bless thyself. Thou met'st with things dying, I with things   100
    new born. Here's a sight for thee! Look thee, a bearing-cloth for
    a squire's child. [*He points to the box*]
    Look thee here! Take up, take up, boy; open't. So; let's see. It was
    told me I should be rich by the fairies. This is some changeling.
    Open't. What's within, boy?   105

CLOWN You're a made old man. If the sins of your youth are forgiven
    you, you're well to live. Gold, all gold!

SHEPHERD This is fairy gold, boy, and 'twill prove so. Up with't, keep
    it close. Home, home, the next way! We are lucky, boy, and to be
    so still requires nothing but secrecy. Let my sheep go. Come,   110
    good boy, the next way home.

CLOWN Go you the next way with your findings. I'll go see if the bear
    be gone from the gentleman, and how much he hath eaten. They
    are never curst but when they are hungry. If there be any of him
    left, I'll bury it.   115

SHEPHERD That's a good deed. If thou mayest discern by that which is
    left of him what he is, fetch me to th'sight of him.

CLOWN Marry, will I; and you shall help to put him i'th'ground.

SHEPHERD 'Tis a lucky day, boy, and we'll do good deeds on't.

Exeunt

Looking back at Act 3
Activities for groups or individuals

1 A message from the gods

Look back at Scene 1 and note all the words and imagery to do with religion. Suggest several reasons why Shakespeare stresses the idea of a holy oracle.

Dion and Cleomenes (carrying the oracle). What do you think the director is trying to achieve in this presentation of the two courtiers?

2 Hot-seating Leontes

Hot-seating is a technique used in drama to explore the motives of a character. In rehearsal for a production it can be a very short informal exercise, where a director asks the actor for in-role motives for an action or movement. When studying a play it can be a useful way of deepening knowledge about a character, as one student steps into role and is questioned by other students.

During Act 3 Leontes suffers the consequences of his delusions, turning from jealous tyranny to grieving repentance. One person volunteers to be Leontes: the rest of the group ask questions about his actions, feelings and motives.

3 Leontes' dream

At the end of Scene 2, Leontes feels deep remorse ('unto/Our shame perpetual'). Imagine he has a dream in which he is accused by Mamillius, Hermione, Polixenes and some courtiers. Prepare a presentation of Leontes' dream, using your own words and quotations from the play. You could use voice-over, chanting, echo, movement, heightened choral speech, music, and so on. You may like to read Shakespeare's version of Richard III's dream the night before his final battle (*Richard III*, Act 5 Scene 3, lines 120–75) where the ghosts of those he has killed return to accuse him.

4 'I am gone for ever!'

Whilst he is obeying Leontes' orders, Antigonus is killed in a particularly horrible way. Does he deserve his fate? Step into role as Antigonus and tell of your loyalty to Leontes, your feelings for the baby, and whether you really believe in Hermione's guilt and that the baby is Polixenes'.

5 From tragedy to comedy

The end of Act 3 forecasts a change of mood from sombre tragedy to light-hearted comedy. Critics often identify lines 100–1 in Scene 3, 'Thou met'st with things dying, I with things new born.' as the turning point of the play (see page 96, Activity 2).

In stage productions directors often change the atmosphere earlier, usually by making the stage direction '*Exit, pursued by a bear*' visually amusing (for example, using an actor in a non-realistic bear costume).

Although a frightening apparition of the bear is justifiable, Shakespeare makes humour clear in the clown's naïve reporting of Antigonus' death, for example, 'nor the bear half dined on the gentleman: he's at it now.' No one knows how Shakespeare himself staged the moment. Perhaps he borrowed a real bear that had been pensioned off from the Bear Pit round the corner from the Globe Theatre!

Decide the point where you would alter the mood of the play, and suggest how you would help to signal it through lighting, music or other stage effects.

Time announces that sixteen years have passed and that Leontes has become a recluse, Polixenes' son is called Florizel, and Perdita is being brought up by the Shepherd in Bohemia.

---

1 Time

The role of Time gives exciting scope for the imagination of both actor and director. Recent interpretations have included:

- Time as a rap artist
- Time descending as a golden feathered bird
- Time's speech written on a scroll inside a balloon which is burst by Camillo who reads the scroll to the audience.

Suggest how you would present Time (an old man with a sickle and hour-glass, a child, a ghostly figure, a clown, or ...?)

2 Speak the lines

Time's speech is written in rhyming couplets (the only occasion when this poetic technique is used for a whole speech in *The Winter's Tale*). Explore different ways of speaking Time's speech. Begin by emphasising the rhymes (see page 214).

3 'Impute it not a crime'

In his *Poetics*, Aristotle said that a well-made play should observe the three unities of time, place and action (the action of the play should take place within 24 hours, all be in one place, and there should be a single unified plot). Shakespeare flouts all the unities in *The Winter's Tale*, and Time shows an awareness of this in lines 4–9.

Write a letter from Shakespeare to a friend justifying his unwillingness to follow Aristotle's advice, and why he uses Time as a chorus to explain the intervening years.

---

try test
unfolds reveals
Impute think
leave the growth untried/Of
  don't explain what's happened to
Let me ... received let me be
  accepted as what I have always
  been, regardless of fashion

turn my glass revolve my
  hourglass
growing development and change
fond foolish
pace hurry
with wond'ring to the admiration
  that she attracts
list not prophesy will not predict

ACT 4   SCENE 1

Enter TIME, the Chorus

TIME   I that please some, try all, both joy and terror
       Of good and bad, that makes and unfolds error,
       Now take upon me, in the name of Time,
       To use my wings. Impute it not a crime
       To me or my swift passage that I slide   5
       O'er sixteen years, and leave the growth untried
       Of that wide gap, since it is in my power
       To o'erthrow law, and in one self-born hour
       To plant and o'erwhelm custom. Let me pass
       The same I am ere ancient'st order was   10
       Or what is now received. I witness to
       The times that brought them in; so shall I do
       To th'freshest things now reigning, and make stale
       The glistering of this present, as my tale
       Now seems to it. Your patience this allowing,   15
       I turn my glass, and give my scene such growing
       As you had slept between. Leontes leaving –
       Th'effects of his fond jealousies so grieving
       That he shuts up himself – imagine me,
       Gentle spectators, that I now may be   20
       In fair Bohemia; and remember well
       I mentioned a son o'th'king's, which Florizel
       I now name to you; and with speed so pace
       To speak of Perdita, now grown in grace
       Equal with wond'ring. What of her ensues   25
       I list not prophesy; but let Time's news
       Be known when 'tis brought forth. A shepherd's daughter
       And what to her adheres, which follows after,
       Is th'argument of Time. Of this allow,
       If ever you have spent time worse ere now;   30
       If never, yet that Time himself doth say
       He wishes earnestly you never may.

                                                          Exit

Camillo wishes to return to Sicilia to comfort the repentant Leontes. Polixenes says Camillo is indispensable in Bohemia. They discuss the absence of Florizel from court and his visits to a shepherd's house.

1 What's been happening? (in pairs)

Scene 2 fills in some of the details which Time did not give about what has happened since Camillo and Polixenes last saw Sicilia. Take parts as Camillo and Polixenes and speak the whole scene. Then list the main developments which have occurred.

2 Pen to paper

In line 5, Camillo tells Polixenes that Leontes has asked him to return to Sicilia. Write the letter that Leontes sends to Camillo. Consider why, now, he has asked Camillo to return. It will be a difficult letter to write after all this time but obviously it must have the desired effect on Camillo.

3 Verse and prose

In Shakespeare it is unusual to find high-ranking people speaking in prose when discussing an important topic. Turn to page 215 and read the section on verse and prose. Then suggest possible reasons why Shakespeare has written Scene 2 in prose.

4 'Eyes under my service'

Polixenes has set spies ('eyes') to keep his son Florizel under surveillance. Keep this information in mind as you read on to help you understand Polixenes' character.

---

importunate demanding
aired breathing the air (exiled)
allay relief
o'erween am too conceited
want (line 10) need

made me begun for me
considered (line 14) rewarded
heaping increasing
missingly regretfully
his removedness where he goes

Bohemia: King Polixenes' palace

Enter POLIXENES and CAMILLO

POLIXENES I pray thee, good Camillo, be no more importunate. 'Tis a
sickness denying thee anything; a death to grant this.

CAMILLO It is fifteen years since I saw my country. Though I have for
the most part been aired abroad, I desire to lay my bones there.
Besides, the penitent king, my master, hath sent for me; to whose   5
feeling sorrows I might be some allay, or I o'erween to think so,
which is another spur to my departure.

POLIXENES As thou lov'st me, Camillo, wipe not out the rest of thy
services by leaving me now. The need I have of thee, thine own
goodness hath made. Better not to have had thee than thus to want   10
thee. Thou, having made me businesses which none without thee
can sufficiently manage, must either stay to execute them thyself or
take away with thee the very services thou hast done; which if I have
not enough considered, as too much I cannot, to be more thankful to
thee shall be my study, and my profit therein the heaping   15
friendships. Of that fatal country Sicilia, prithee speak no more,
whose very naming punishes me with the remembrance of that
penitent, as thou call'st him, and reconciled king, my brother; whose
loss of his most precious queen and children are even now to be
afresh lamented. Say to me, when saw'st thou the Prince Florizel my   20
son? Kings are no less unhappy, their issue not being gracious, than
they are in losing them when they have approved their virtues.

CAMILLO Sir, it is three days since I saw the prince. What his happier
affairs may be are to me unknown; but I have missingly noted he
is of late much retired from court, and is less frequent to his   25
princely exercises than formerly he hath appeared.

POLIXENES I have considered so much, Camillo, and with some care –
so far, that I have eyes under my service which look upon his
removedness, from whom I have this intelligence, that he is
seldom from the house of a most homely shepherd – a man, they   30
say, that from very nothing, and beyond the imagination of his
neighbours, is grown into an unspeakable estate.

Camillo tells of the Shepherd's beautiful daughter. Polixenes fears the daughter will entrap Florizel. He plans to visit her home in disguise. Autolycus enters, singing about stealing.

'Tirra-lirra'. What do the words of Autolycus' songs in lines 1–22 suggest about his way of life?

intelligence information	**pale** faded colours, or, fenced-off area
angle fish hook	
uneasy difficult	**pugging ... edge** thieving nature to work
resort thither visits there	
doxy beggar's girlfriend	**aunts** girlfriends, whores
red blood sexual desires	

CAMILLO I have heard, sir, of such a man, who hath a daughter of most
    rare note. The report of her is extended more than can be thought
    to begin from such a cottage.   35
POLIXENES That's likewise part of my intelligence; but, I fear, the angle
    that plucks our son thither. Thou shalt accompany us to the place,
    where we will, not appearing what we are, have some question
    with the shepherd; from whose simplicity I think it not uneasy to
    get the cause of my son's resort thither. Prithee be my present   40
    partner in this business, and lay aside the thoughts of Sicilia.
CAMILLO I willingly obey your command.
POLIXENES My best Camillo! We must disguise ourselves.

                                                    [*Exeunt*]

ACT 4   SCENE 3
Bohemia: a country road

Enter AUTOLYCUS singing

AUTOLYCUS   When daffodils begin to peer,
                With heigh the doxy over the dale,
            Why then comes in the sweet o'the year,
                For the red blood reigns in the winter's pale.

            The white sheet bleaching on the hedge,   5
                With heigh the sweet birds, O how they sing!
            Doth set my pugging tooth an edge,
                For a quart of ale is a dish for a king.

            The lark, that tirra-lirra chants,
                With heigh, with heigh, the thrush and the jay,   10
            Are summer songs for me and my aunts
                While we lie tumbling in the hay.

Autolycus says he used to serve Prince Florizel but now he is a thief. The Shepherd's son enters with a list of things to buy for the sheep-shearing feast. Autolycus prepares to rob him.

1 A born thief (in pairs)

Autolycus calls himself a 'snapper-up of unconsidered trifles' (line 25). In classical mythology Autolycus, a son of Mercury, the god of trading, stole sheep from his neighbours' flocks and mixed them with his own. Shakespeare's Autolycus attributes his father's thieving habits and his own to the fact that they were both born ('littered') under the star sign of Mercury. He says he steals underwear ('lesser linen') in spring 'when the kite builds' his nest, and that his rough outfit is the result of gambling and whoring ('die and drab'). He makes his living from cheating the simple-minded.

Take it in turns to perform Autolycus' lines 23–9. Experiment! What is the effect of speaking to the audience? to yourself? to a pocket mirror? to individual members of the audience, possibly attempting to 'steal' from them? Or …?

2 Shopping for the feast (in pairs)

The Clown is trying to work out the profit from the sheep-shearing. He knows that every eleven sheep yield twenty-eight pounds of wool ('every 'leven wether tods' – a tod is 28 lb), but he cannot work out how much they have earned from the whole flock. He is shopping for his sister, who is preparing food for the feast. Autolycus thinks the Clown is as stupid as a woodcock, a bird reputedly very easy to catch in a trap ('springe').

Speak the Clown's lines to extract as much humour as possible from them.

---

three-pile expensive thick velvet
tinkers menders of kettles, etc.
bear the sow-skin budget carry their pigskin tool bag
avouch it claim I'm a tinker (to avoid punishment)
caparison outfit

Gallows and knock hanging and thrashing
means and basses tenor and bass voices
warden pear
raisins o'th'sun sun-dried grapes

I have served Prince Florizel, and in my time wore three-pile,
but now I am out of service.

> But shall I go mourn for that, my dear?　　　　　15
> 　The pale moon shines by night;
> And when I wander here and there,
> 　I then do most go right.

> If tinkers may have leave to live,
> 　And bear the sow-skin budget,　　　　　20
> Then my account I well may give,
> 　And in the stocks avouch it.

My traffic is sheets; when the kite builds, look to lesser linen. My
father named me Autolycus, who being, as I am, littered under
Mercury, was likewise a snapper-up of unconsidered trifles. With　　25
die and drab I purchased this caparison, and my revenue is the
silly cheat. Gallows and knock are too powerful on the highway.
Beating and hanging are terrors to me. For the life to come, I sleep
out the thought of it. A prize, a prize!

Enter CLOWN

CLOWN Let me see, every 'leven wether tods, every tod yields pound　　30
and odd shilling; fifteen hundred shorn, what comes the wool to?
AUTOLYCUS [*Aside*] If the springe hold, the cock's mine.
CLOWN I cannot do't without counters. Let me see, what am I to buy
for our sheep-shearing feast? Three pound of sugar, five pound of
currants, rice – what will this sister of mine do with rice? But my　　35
father hath made her mistress of the feast, and she lays it on. She
hath made me four-and-twenty nosegays for the shearers –
three-man song-men all, and very good ones – but they are most
of them means and basses; but one puritan amongst them, and he
sings psalms to hornpipes. I must have saffron to colour the　　40
warden pies; mace; dates – none, that's out of my note; nutmegs,
seven; a race or two of ginger – but that I may beg; four pound of
prunes, and as many of raisins o'th'sun.

*Autolycus fools the Shepherd's son into believing that he has been
attacked and robbed. The Clown helps Autolycus to stand up and
Autolycus picks his pocket.*

1 A con man at work (in pairs)

Autolycus has overheard the Clown say that he has money for buying
spices. He intends to steal it. Take parts and act out the encounter
between the Clown and Autolycus (lines 44–102). Bring out as much
humour as you can. The following points can help your preparation:

- will Autolycus use a different accent from the one he uses when
  he is alone?

- how does he play a badly injured man?

- work on the implicit stage directions at lines 68–72 where
  Shakespeare gives Autolycus lines to prevent his theft of the
  clown's money being discovered.

- what else might Autolycus steal? One production had him
  audaciously riding off on the clown's bicycle.

2 Master pedlar: Autolycus? Shakespeare?

Below, and continued on page 110, is Louis MacNeice's poem,
'Autolycus', which explores the nature of Shakespeare's Late Plays.
Consider what MacNeice might have had in mind when he equates
Shakespeare with Autolycus ('O master pedlar') in his poem. Page 204
can help you.

> In his last phase when hardly bothering
> To be a dramatist, the Master turned away
> From his taught plots and complex characters
> To tapestried romances, conjuring
> With rainbow names and handfuls of sea-spray
> And from them turned out happy Ever-afters.

---

stripes scars from whipping
apparel tane clothes stolen
horseman mounted highwayman
footman footpad, mugger

troll-my-dames a game of rolling
a ball through holes (a punning
reference to loose women)
no more but abide soon leave

AUTOLYCUS [*Grovelling on the ground*] O that ever I was born!

CLOWN I'th'name of me!   45

AUTOLYCUS O, help me, help me! Pluck but off these rags, and then
    death, death!

CLOWN Alack, poor soul, thou hast need of more rags to lay on thee,
    rather than have these off.

AUTOLYCUS O sir, the loathsomeness of them offend me more than the   50
    stripes I have received, which are mighty ones and millions.

CLOWN Alas, poor man, a million of beating may come to a great
    matter.

AUTOLYCUS I am robbed, sir, and beaten; my money and apparel tane
    from me, and these detestable things put upon me.   55

CLOWN What, by a horseman or a footman?

AUTOLYCUS A footman, sweet sir, a footman.

CLOWN Indeed, he should be a footman, by the garments he has left
    with thee. If this be a horseman's coat, it hath seen very hot service.
    Lend me thy hand, I'll help thee. Come, lend me thy hand.   60

[*He helps him up*]

AUTOLYCUS O, good sir, tenderly, O!

CLOWN Alas, poor soul!

AUTOLYCUS O, good sir, softly, good sir! I fear, sir, my shoulder-blade
    is out.

CLOWN How now? Canst stand?   65

AUTOLYCUS [*Picking his pocket*] Softly, dear sir; good sir, softly. You
    ha' done me a charitable office.

CLOWN Dost lack any money? I have a little money for thee.

AUTOLYCUS No, good sweet sir; no, I beseech you, sir. I have a kinsman
    not past three-quarters of a mile hence, unto whom I was going.   70
    I shall there have money, or anything I want. Offer me no money,
    I pray you; that kills my heart.

CLOWN What manner of fellow was he that robbed you?

AUTOLYCUS A fellow, sir, that I have known to go about with troll-
    my-dames. I knew him once a servant of the prince. I cannot tell,   75
    good sir, for which of his virtues it was, but he was certainly
    whipped out of the court.

CLOWN His vices, you would say; there's no virtue whipped out of the
    court. They cherish it to make it stay there; and yet it will no more
    but abide.   80

Autolycus says his attacker is called Autolycus. The Clown replies
that he has heard of him and that he is a thief and a coward.
Autolycus plans to rob others at the sheep-shearing.

'Autolycus' by Louis MacNeice, continued from page 108

Eclectic always, now extravagant,
Sighting his matter through a timeless prison
He ranged his classical bric-a-brac in grottos
Where knights of Ancient Greece had Latin mottoes
And fishermen their flap-jacks – none should want
Colour for lack of an anachronism.

A gay world certainly though pocked and scored
With childish horrors and a fresh world though
Its mainsprings were old gags – babies exposed
Identities confused and queens to be restored;
But when the cracker bursts it proves as you supposed –
Trinket and moral tumble out just so.

Such innocence – In his own words it was
Like an old tale, only that where time leaps
Between acts three and four there was something born
Which made the stock-type virgin dance like corn
In a wind that having known foul marshes, barren steeps,
Felt therefore kindly towards Marinas, Perditas.

Thus crystal learned to talk. But Shakespeare balanced it
With what we knew already, gabbing earth
Hot from Eastcheap – Watch your pockets when
That rogue comes round the corner, he can slit
Purse strings as quickly as his maker's pen
Will try your heart-strings in the name of mirth.

O master pedlar with your confidence tricks,
Brooches, pomanders, broad sheets and what-have-you
Who hawk such entertainment but rook your client
And leave him brooding, why should we forgive you
Did we not know that, though more self-reliant
Than we, you too were born and grew up in a fix?

---

ape-bearer showman with
  performing monkey
process court summonses
compassed a motion managed a
  travelling puppet show
land and living estate
Prig thief

wakes funerals or festivals
false of heart faint-hearted
hot enough full of money
cheat bring out theft lead to
unrolled removed from the list of
  rogues
hent leap over

AUTOLYCUS Vices I would say, sir. I know this man well. He hath been since an ape-bearer; then a process-server, a bailiff; then he compassed a motion of the Prodigal Son, and married a tinker's wife within a mile where my land and living lies; and having flown over many knavish professions, he settled only in rogue. Some call   85
him Autolycus.

CLOWN Out upon him! Prig, for my life, prig! He haunts wakes, fairs and bear-baitings.

AUTOLYCUS Very true, sir; he, sir, he: that's the rogue that put me into this apparel.   90

CLOWN Not a more cowardly rogue in all Bohemia. If you had but looked big and spit at him, he'd have run.

AUTOLYCUS I must confess to you, sir, I am no fighter. I am false of heart that way, and that he knew, I warrant him.

CLOWN How do you now?   95

AUTOLYCUS Sweet sir, much better than I was. I can stand and walk. I will even take my leave of you, and pace softly towards my kinsman's.

CLOWN Shall I bring thee on the way?

AUTOLYCUS No, good-faced sir; no, sweet sir.   100

CLOWN Then fare thee well; I must go buy spices for our sheep-shearing.   *Exit*

AUTOLYCUS Prosper you, sweet sir! Your purse is not hot enough to purchase your spice. I'll be with you at your sheep-shearing too. If I make not this cheat bring out another, and the shearers prove   105
sheep, let me be unrolled and my name put in the book of virtue.

[*He sings*]

> Jog on, jog on, the footpath way,
>   And merrily hent the stile-a;
> A merry heart goes all the day,
>   Your sad tires in a mile-a.   *Exit*   110

Florizel praises Perdita: her costume displays her beauty.
Perdita is embarrassed by her appearance as a queen. Florizel remembers
with joy their initial meeting, but Perdita fears discovery.

1 A play within a play (in small groups)

Florizel and Perdita are preparing for the sheep-shearing festival.
Perdita is dressed as the queen of the feast ('Most goddess-like pranked
up') and Florizel, the prince, is disguised as a shepherd or peasant
('obscured/With a swain's wearing'). Discuss how you would ensure
that the audience understand that Florizel is a prince, playing a
peasant, and that Perdita is a shepherdess playing queen of the feast.
(Remember that she really is a princess, the daughter of King Leontes.)

2 First meeting (in pairs)

Use the information given in lines 14–16 to improvise the first meeting
between Florizel and Perdita.

3 Differences in social class

The difference in social class is frequently mentioned opposite. Perdita
calls Florizel 'The gracious mark o'th'land' compared to herself, 'poor
lowly maid'. She fears the 'difference' (line 17) between them, afraid
that the king may discover his son, 'Vilely bound up' (dressed as a
peasant, or wrapped in the arms of a shepherdess). As you read on you
will find that the question of differences in social class is an important
issue in the play.

Make your suggestion about why Perdita, a shepherdess, speaks in
verse not prose. If you need help, turn to page 215.

---

unusual weeds special clothes
Flora goddess of spring
Peering in April's front
  appearing in advance of the spring
petty lesser

extremes high praise
But that our ... custom if it were
  not for the fact that everyone at
  feasts enjoys foolishness, treating it
  as customary
flaunts elaborate clothes

Act 4 Scene 4
Bohemia: near the Shepherd's cottage

Enter FLORIZEL *and* PERDITA

FLORIZEL These your unusual weeds to each part of you
        Does give a life: no shepherdess, but Flora
        Peering in April's front. This your sheep-shearing
        Is as a meeting of the petty gods,
        And you the queen on't.
PERDITA   Sir, my gracious lord,   5
        To chide at your extremes it not becomes me –
        O, pardon that I name them! Your high self,
        The gracious mark o'th'land, you have obscured
        With a swain's wearing, and me, poor lowly maid,
        Most goddess-like pranked up. But that our feasts   10
        In every mess have folly, and the feeders
        Digest it with a custom, I should blush
        To see you so attired; swoon, I think,
        To show myself a glass.
FLORIZEL   I bless the time
        When my good falcon made her flight across   15
        Thy father's ground.
PERDITA   Now Jove afford you cause!
        To me the difference forges dread; your greatness
        Hath not been used to fear. Even now I tremble
        To think your father by some accident
        Should pass this way, as you did. O, the Fates!   20
        How would he look to see his work, so noble,
        Vilely bound up? What would he say? Or how
        Should I, in these my borrowed flaunts, behold
        The sternness of his presence?

Florizel compares his courtship of Perdita to that of the gods wooing mortal maidens. He insists that his love is virtuous. Perdita fears that discovery by the king will end their love and her life.

1 Dubious comparisons

Florizel compares the fact that he has disguised himself as a simple shepherd to the various ways that gods in mythology disguised themselves. The gods also chose to disguise themselves for love, but their motive was usually seduction:

- Jupiter, the most powerful god, changed himself into a bull to seduce Europa.
- Neptune, god of the sea, changed into many different forms, including a ram, to seduce Theopane.
- Apollo, the sun god, was a shepherd for nine years after being exiled for killing the Cyclops.

Florizel claims that his love is chaste, and his intentions strictly honourable. Florizel is trying to reassure Perdita of the purity of his love, but his choice of gods is perhaps unfortunate!

2 Dawn of young love

In the second half of the play, there is comedy to oppose the tragedy of the first half, and also young committed love which contrasts sharply with Leontes' jealous fury. As you read on, notice how often Florizel and Perdita mention their devotion to one another.

Apprehend expect
deities nature as gods
piece ... rarer more beautiful
 woman

One ... necessities one of these
 two things must happen
forced unnatural
gentle sweetheart
auspicious favourable

FLORIZEL   Apprehend
　　　Nothing but jollity. The gods themselves,   25
　　　Humbling their deities to love, have taken
　　　The shapes of beasts upon them: Jupiter
　　　Became a bull, and bellowed; the green Neptune
　　　A ram, and bleated; and the fire-robed god,
　　　Golden Apollo, a poor humble swain,   30
　　　As I seem now. Their transformations
　　　Were never for a piece of beauty rarer.
　　　Nor in a way so chaste, since my desires
　　　Run not before mine honour, nor my lusts
　　　Burn hotter than my faith.
PERDITA   O, but sir,   35
　　　Your resolution cannot hold when 'tis
　　　Opposed, as it must be, by th'power of the king.
　　　One of these two must be necessities,
　　　Which then will speak, that you must change this purpose,
　　　Or I my life.
FLORIZEL   Thou dearest Perdita,   40
　　　With these forced thoughts, I prithee, darken not
　　　The mirth o'th'feast. Or I'll be thine, my fair,
　　　Or not my father's; for I cannot be
　　　Mine own, nor anything to any, if
　　　I be not thine. To this I am most constant,   45
　　　Though destiny say no. Be merry, gentle;
　　　Strangle such thoughts as these with anything
　　　That you behold the while. Your guests are coming;
　　　Lift up your countenance as it were the day
　　　Of celebration of that nuptial which   50
　　　We two have sworn shall come.
PERDITA   O Lady Fortune,
　　　Stand you auspicious!
FLORIZEL   See, your guests approach.
　　　Address yourself to entertain them sprightly,
　　　And let's be red with mirth.

The guests arrive for the feast. The Shepherd rebukes Perdita for being too shy. He says his late wife was a better hostess. Perdita offers herbs to the disguised Polixenes and Camillo.

1 Staging the entry (in large groups)

The entrance of a number of actors is a fascinating challenge for the director. Try several ways of rehearsing the entrance of the guests to the feast. You might, for example, want to echo the entrance of the court in Act 1. Do the guests bring on any of the props for the feast? Work out how to draw attention to the disguised Polixenes and Camillo to ensure that the audience recognises them.

2 'My old wife'

Step into role as the Shepherd's wife. Using lines 55–62, write an account of a feast at which she was present.

3 'A fair one are you'

Polixenes suspects that Perdita has trapped his son. Speak his private thoughts when he sees her, before he speaks to her at line 78. In what tone does he say 'Shepherdess'?

4 The language of flowers

Through the centuries flowers and herbs have been used to symbolise emotions. Perdita offers Polixenes and Camillo rosemary and rue, which represent remembrance and bitter repentance (though rue is also called the 'herb of grace'). Why do you think that Shakespeare felt that these were suitable herbs to be offered to Polixenes and Camillo? As you read on you will find that Perdita refers to many other flowers with their appropriate symbolism in mind.

---

pantler servant in charge of the pantry
butler servant in charge of wine
dame mistress of the household
retired holding back

feasted one person in whose honour the feast is held
quench your blushes stop being shy
Seeming and savour appearance and scent

[*Enter* SHEPHERD, CLOWN, POLIXENES *and* CAMILLO *in disguise;*
MOPSA, DORCAS, *and others*]

SHEPHERD Fie, daughter! When my old wife lived, upon   55
        This day she was both pantler, butler, cook,
        Both dame and servant, welcomed all, served all,
        Would sing her song and dance her turn, now here,
        At upper end o'th'table, now i'th'middle,
        On his shoulder, and his, her face o'fire   60
        With labour, and the thing she took to quench it
        She would to each one sip. You are retired,
        As if you were a feasted one and not
        The hostess of the meeting. Pray you bid
        These unknown friends to's welcome, for it is   65
        A way to make us better friends, more known.
        Come, quench your blushes and present yourself
        That which you are, Mistress o'th'Feast. Come on,
        And bid us welcome to your sheep-shearing,
        As your good flock shall prosper.
PERDITA [*To Polixenes*]   Sir, welcome.   70
        It is my father's will I should take on me
        The hostess-ship o'th'day. [*To Camillo*] You're welcome, sir.
        Give me those flowers there, Dorcas. Reverend sirs,
        For you there's rosemary and rue; these keep
        Seeming and savour all the winter long.   75
        Grace and remembrance be to you both,
        And welcome to our shearing!
POLIXENES   Shepherdess –
        A fair one are you – well you fit our ages
        With flowers of winter.

Perdita says that she has no carnations to offer her guests. She says that they are the result of grafting and that she prefers not to meddle with nature. Polixenes argues in favour of grafting.

1 Nature *versus* nurture (in small groups)

Polixenes explains that he approves of the cross-breeding of plants because gardeners can improve on nature only by following the laws of nature; to do so is an art. Poor quality plants ('the wildest stock') can be improved by grafting on 'A gentler scion' (a higher quality cutting). This is an example of dramatic irony because Polixenes does not approve of his son, the prince, marrying a low-status woman (whom he also thinks of as 'wildest stock').

Perdita seems to agree with Polixenes' argument: 'So it is'. Perhaps she is thinking of her relationship with Florizel because she continues to argue against the cross-breeding of plants. She rejects Polixenes' argument, saying it is as false as if Florizel were to love her only because she was heavily made up with cosmetics ('were I painted').

a Suggest the arguments you think Polixenes would give against the marriage of Perdita and Florizel, in spite of his support for the grafting of plants.

b Talk together about the relative importance of heredity and upbringing. What might happen if a baby from a very poor family were adopted by a very high-status family?

c The argument between Polixenes and Perdita is very relevant today because advances in science and medicine have made it possible to 'graft' human beings. Widen your discussion to include the topics of transplant surgery, *in vitro* fertilisation and genetic engineering.

---

gillyvors pinks (small carnations)	**mean** method
slips cuttings	**bark** plant
piedness mixed colour	**dibble** small trowel

PERDITA   Sir, the year growing ancient,
    Not yet on summer's death nor on the birth   80
    Of trembling winter, the fairest flowers o'th'season
    Are our carnations and streaked gillyvors,
    Which some call nature's bastards. Of that kind
    Our rustic garden's barren, and I care not
    To get slips of them.
POLIXENES   Wherefore, gentle maiden,   85
    Do you neglect them?
PERDITA   For I have heard it said
    There is an art which in their piedness shares
    With great creating nature.
POLIXENES   Say there be,
    Yet nature is made better by no mean
    But nature makes that mean; so over that art,   90
    Which you say adds to nature, is an art
    That nature makes. You see, sweet maid, we marry
    A gentler scion to the wildest stock,
    And make conceive a bark of baser kind
    By bud of nobler race. This is an art   95
    Which does mend nature – change it rather – but
    The art itself is nature.
PERDITA   So it is.
POLIXENES Then make your garden rich in gillyvors,
    And do not call them bastards.
PERDITA   I'll not put
    The dibble in earth to set one slip of them;   100
    No more than, were I painted, I would wish
    This youth should say 'twere well, and only therefore
    Desire to breed by me. Here's flowers for you:
    Hot lavender, mints, savory, marjoram;
    The marigold, that goes to bed wi'th'sun   105
    And with him rises weeping. These are flowers
    Of middle summer, and I think they are given
    To men of middle age. Y'are very welcome.

Camillo admires Perdita. She offers appropriate flowers to the young shepherdesses and describes the flowers she would like to have in order to make garlands for them and Florizel.

1 Perdita's flowers: symbolism and sound

The story of Proserpina (lines 116–18) is a myth about the seasons of the year. Proserpina was the daughter of Jupiter and Ceres. Dis (or Pluto), god of the Underworld, was infatuated with her. He saw her picking flowers one day and as he carried her off to his kingdom, she dropped her flowers.

Because she ate pomegranate seeds in the Underworld, Prosperina was allowed back to earth for only six months of each year. In misery at her absence, Ceres, goddess of harvests, decreed that crops should grow during only half the year. Using this myth, some critics have seen Perdita as a symbolic awakening after the long winter of Leontes' madness and grief.

Many people have argued that Shakespeare provides the actor with language which matches sound to meaning. They point to the use of soft sibilant (S) and labial (L) sounds in the passage describing flowers (for example, 'thou let'st fall/From Dis's wagon'). Speak lines 112–29 (from 'Now, my fair'st friend'), then think about whether the sounds affect your understanding of the speech, and your feelings about it.

2 Do clothes change behaviour? (in small groups)

Pastorals were small entertainments performed at Whitsun, for example, plays about Robin Hood. The actors wore elaborate costumes. Perdita suggests that the garments she is wearing as queen of the festival are influencing her behaviour ('change my disposition').

Use Perdita's lines 134–5 to discuss whether your behaviour changes when you wear different clothes. If possible, experiment with costumes available in your drama wardrobe.

Juno queen of the gods
Cytherea Venus, goddess of love
Phoebus … strength sun in summer

malady/Most incident to maids green sickness, most common in unmarried girls (such girls who died were believed to turn into primroses)
corse dead body
quick alive
Whitsun seven weeks after Easter (usually late May)

CAMILLO   I should leave grazing, were I of your flock,
　　　　　And only live by gazing.
PERDITA　　　　　　　　　　　Out, alas!   110
　　　　　You'd be so lean that blasts of January
　　　　　Would blow you through and through. [*To Florizel*] Now,
　　　　　my fair'st friend,
　　　　　I would I had some flowers o'th'spring that might
　　　　　Become your time of day – [*To Shepherdesses*] and yours,
　　　　　and yours,
　　　　　That wear upon your virgin branches yet   115
　　　　　Your maidenheads growing. O Proserpina,
　　　　　For the flowers now that, frighted, thou let'st fall
　　　　　From Dis's waggon! Daffodils,
　　　　　That come before the swallow dares, and take
　　　　　The winds of March with beauty; violets, dim,   120
　　　　　But sweeter than the lids of Juno's eyes
　　　　　Or Cytherea's breath; pale primroses,
　　　　　That die unmarried ere they can behold
　　　　　Bright Phoebus in his strength – a malady
　　　　　Most incident to maids; bold oxlips, and   125
　　　　　The crown imperial; lilies of all kinds,
　　　　　The flower-de-luce being one. O, these I lack
　　　　　To make you garlands of, and my sweet friend,
　　　　　To strew him o'er and o'er!
FLORIZEL　　　　　　　　　　　What, like a corse?
PERDITA   No, like a bank for love to lie and play on,   130
　　　　　Not like a corse; or if, not to be buried,
　　　　　But quick and in mine arms. Come, take your flowers.
　　　　　Methinks I play as I have seen them do
　　　　　In Whitsun pastorals; sure this robe of mine
　　　　　Does change my disposition.

Florizel speaks of Perdita's perfection. She clears him of false flattery.
Polixenes and Camillo also praise her. Dorcas says Mopsa must dance
with the Shepherd's son. The dance begins.

1 Improving perfection (in pairs)

For his secret wooing of Perdita, Florizel has assumed the name of
Doricles. In lines 135–46 he says that every action of Perdita's improves
on what she has done before.

a Speak the lines slowly to one another, twice, listening for the
  rhythm in the lines. Lightly stress words to do with action.

b Use the lines to present a movement sequence for Florizel and
  Perdita where each mirrors the other's movements.

c Some critics have claimed that these lines are among the very best
  that Shakespeare wrote. What special qualities do you find in
  them?

2 'So turtles pair ...'

Turtle doves (line 154) were often used in poetry to represent life-long
love because they were believed to mate for life. Suggest one other
image Florizel might have used to express his devotion to Perdita.

3 'Come on, strike up!'

The Clown calls the band to play before a quarrel between Mopsa and
Dorcas develops. You will discover that the girls argue later. In lines
162–3, Dorcas says that Mopsa must dance with the Clown (why?), and
implies that she has bad breath that needs garlic to improve it.

Suggest what kind of dance you would stage, and whether the
quarrel invades it (one production had Dorcas stamping on the clown's
foot each time they met in the dance).

Each your doing everything
  you do
in the present deeds at the
  moment
true blood noble birth
unstained innocent

greensward grass
blood look out blush
strike up! start playing the music
stand ... manners are on our best
  behaviour

FLORIZEL   What you do   135
  Still betters what is done. When you speak, sweet,
  I'd have you do it ever; when you sing,
  I'd have you buy and sell so, so give alms,
  Pray so, and, for the ord'ring your affairs,
  To sing them too. When you do dance, I wish you   140
  A wave o'th'sea, that you might ever do
  Nothing but that – move still, still so,
  And own no other function. Each your doing,
  So singular in each particular,
  Crowns what you are doing in the present deeds,   145
  That all your acts are queens.
PERDITA   O Doricles,
  Your praises are too large. But that your youth
  And the true blood which peeps fairly through't
  Do plainly give you out an unstained shepherd,
  With wisdom I might fear, my Doricles,   150
  You wooed me the false way.
FLORIZEL   I think you have
  As little skill to fear as I have purpose
  To put you to't. But come, our dance, I pray.
  Your hand, my Perdita: so turtles pair
  That never mean to part.
PERDITA   I'll swear for 'em.   155
POLIXENES [*To Camillo*] This is the prettiest low-born lass that ever
  Ran on the greensward. Nothing she does or seems
  But smacks of something greater than herself,
  Too noble for this place.
CAMILLO   He tells her something
  That makes her blood look out. Good sooth, she is   160
  The queen of curds and cream.
CLOWN   Come on, strike up!
DORCAS Mopsa must be your mistress. Marry, garlic
  To mend her kissing with!
MOPSA   Now, in good time!
CLOWN Not a word, a word; we stand upon our manners.
  Come, strike up!   165

  [*Music.*] *Here a dance of Shepherds and Shepherdesses*

The Shepherd tells Polixenes that if Doricles (Florizel) marries Perdita she will bring a surprising dowry. The Servant says a pedlar has arrived bringing a whole range of love ballads.

1 Dramatic irony, dramatic direction

The Shepherd seems proud of his daughter and her suitor, reporting Doricles' claim to have a high-status family ('boasts himself/To have a worthy feeding'). He describes their equality of love for one another ('not half a kiss to choose/Who loves another best'). Because the Shepherd is talking to Polixenes, who the audience knows is Doricles/Florizel's father, dramatic irony intensifies the humour and tension of the scene.

a How can Polixenes add to the dramatic irony in the way he speaks his three words at line 176? Suggest his tone of voice and his expression.

b In lines 172–4, the Shepherd describes how Doricles/Florizel looks at Perdita. If you were directing Florizel, at which point in this scene would you want him to use this information?

2 Speak as the Servant

The Servant reports that the pedlar has ballads for sale. Ballads were popular, very like pop music today. The Servant gives a confused account of the songs. He says they are 'without bawdry' (not dirty songs), but proceeds to describe all the naughty bits; like 'jump her and thump her', 'dildos' (phalluses) and 'fadings' (a kind of dance, or a chorus from an indecent song).

You have been chosen to play the Servant. You have only lines 181–5, 189–96 and 200–5. Work out how you are going to make the most of your role, then deliver your lines.

---

like sooth truthful	**lamentably** sadly, badly
featly gracefully	**delicate burdens** pretty choruses
light upon marry	**stretched-mouthed** loud mouthed
tabor small drum	**foul gap** improvised naughty bit
tell money count cash	**slights** stops
doleful sad	**unbraided** new, not faded

POLIXENES Pray, good shepherd, what fair swain is this
    Which dances with your daughter?
SHEPHERD They call him Doricles, and boasts himself
    To have a worthy feeding; but I have it
    Upon his own report, and I believe it: 170
    He looks like sooth. He says he loves my daughter.
    I think so too, for never gazed the moon
    Upon the water as he'll stand and read,
    As 'twere, my daughter's eyes; and, to be plain,
    I think there is not half a kiss to choose   175
    Who loves another best.
POLIXENES   She dances featly.
SHEPHERD So she does anything, though I report it
    That should be silent. If young Doricles
    Do light upon her, she shall bring him that
    Which he not dreams of.   180

Enter SERVANT

SERVANT O master, if you did but hear the pedlar at the door you would
    never dance again after a tabor and pipe; no, the bagpipe could not
    move you. He sings several tunes faster than you'll tell money; he
    utters them as he had eaten ballads and all men's ears grew to his
    tunes.   185
CLOWN He could never come better. He shall come in. I love a ballad
    but even too well, if it be doleful matter merrily set down, or a very
    pleasant thing indeed and sung lamentably.
SERVANT He hath songs for man or woman, of all sizes; no milliner can
    so fit his customers with gloves. He has the prettiest love-songs   190
    for maids, so without bawdry, which is strange, with such delicate
    burdens of dildos and fadings, 'jump her and thump her'; and
    where some stretch-mouthed rascal would, as it were, mean mis-
    chief and break a foul gap into the matter, he makes the maid to
    answer, 'Whoop, do me no harm, good man'; puts him off, slights   195
    him, with 'Whoop, do me no harm, good man.'
POLIXENES This is a brave fellow.
CLOWN Believe me, thou talkest of an admirable conceited fellow. Has
    he any unbraided wares?

The Servant describes all the dressmaking items the pedlar has in his pack. Autolycus sings about his wares. Mopsa and Dorcas quarrel and the Clown quietens them.

1 What's in Autolycus' pack?

The Servant makes Autolycus' pack sound as though it is crammed with goods. He begins by describing items which everyone would know and need to buy – 'ribbons' and 'points' (laces for tying garments) – and makes a pun about legal 'points' (questions) coming wholesale – 'by th'gross'. He then launches into a list: 'inkles' (linen tapes), 'caddisses' (worsted tapes), 'cambrics' (fabric), 'lawns' (fine linen). Finally, the Servant suggests that Autolycus is able to make 'a smock' sound blessed because he 'chants' about the work in the 'sleevehand' (cuff) and the 'square' (which covered the chest).

Autolycus sensuously describes more goods in his song. 'Lawn' and 'Cypress' (types of expensive fabric), perfumed gloves, masks and jewellery, all sound like wares for the nobility, rather than for the shepherds and shepherdesses. Present Autolycus' song in a way you think he would use (for example, sexy and suggestive). You don't necessarily have to sing the lines.

2 Stopping a quarrel (in groups of three)

Lines 223–36 offer many opportunities for lively action on stage. What is Mopsa suggesting about the previous relationship between Dorcas and the Clown? How does the Clown rebuke the quarrelling shepherdesses? What might he do as he speaks 'plackets' (line 232: a placket was an opening in a skirt or petticoat – often used as a euphemism for the vagina)? Take parts and make it as entertaining as you can.

---

scurrilous rude
Bugle-bracelet bracelet of black glass beads
coifs tightly fitting caps
stomachers front piece of a dress, ending in a point

poking-sticks rods to poke the folds in a neck-ruff evenly
against before
kill-hole warm hole by the fire in a baking kiln; a place for gossip
Clamor silence

SERVANT He hath ribbons of all the colours i'th'rainbow; points more   200
than all the lawyers in Bohemia can learnedly handle, though they
come to him by th'gross; inkles, caddisses, cambrics, lawns. Why,
he sings 'em over as they were gods or goddesses; you would think
a smock were a she-angel, he so chants to the sleevehand and the
work about the square on't.   205

CLOWN Prithee bring him in, and let him approach singing.

PERDITA Forewarn him that he use no scurrilous words in's tunes.

[*Exit Servant*]

CLOWN You have of these pedlars that have more in them than you'd
think, sister.

PERDITA Ay, good brother, or go about to think.   210

Enter AUTOLYCUS *singing*

AUTOLYCUS   Lawn as white as driven snow,
Cypress black as e'er was crow,
Gloves as sweet as damask roses,
Masks for faces and for noses,
Bugle-bracelet, necklace amber,   215
Perfume for a lady's chamber,
Golden coifs and stomachers
For my lads to give their dears,
Pins and poking-sticks of steel –
What maids lack from head to heel.   220
    Come buy of me, come, come buy, come buy;
    Buy, lads, or else your lasses cry: Come buy!

CLOWN If I were not in love with Mopsa thou shouldst take no money
of me, but being enthralled as I am, it will also be the bondage of
certain ribbons and gloves.   225

MOPSA I was promised them against the feast, but they come not too
late now.

DORCAS He hath promised you more than that, or there be liars.

MOPSA He hath paid you all he promised you; may be he has paid you
more, which will shame you to give him again.   230

CLOWN Is there no manners left among maids? Will they wear their
plackets where they should bear their faces? Is there not
milking-time, when you are going to bed, or kill-hole, to whistle of
these secrets, but you must be tittle-tattling before all our guests?
'Tis well they are whisp'ring. Clamor your tongues, and not a word   235
more.

Mopsa wants the Clown to buy her gifts. Autolycus fools the shepherds and shepherdesses by telling them that the fantastic stories told in his ballads are true.

1 'Tawdry-lace': St Audrey's lace

A 'tawdry-lace' (line 236) was a silk necktie. Audrey, a Christian saint, developed a throat tumour which she believed was a punishment for her vanity in wearing fancy neckerchiefs. It is ironic that her name became connected to elaborate neckties and lace for the throat. Look up the word 'tawdry' in a large dictionary in a library to discover how its meaning still echoes St Audrey's story.

2 Autolycus' conscience (in groups of five)

Imagine that Autolycus has a conscience, visible at his shoulder. Take parts as Autolycus, his conscience, Mopsa, Dorcas and the Clown and speak lines 237–79. As Autolycus speaks his lines, his conscience comments on what he says. This is a useful exercise for an actor playing Autolycus as he needs to convey to the audience that he is well aware of his own con tricks.

3 Ballads

Ballads, the popular songs of their day, were like tabloid newspapers today in telling colourful and outlandish stories. Autolycus' first ballad is about the wife of a money-lender (usurer) who gave birth to twenty bags of money on one occasion. Like many pregnant women she had strange fancies about food, longing to eat grilled adders' heads and toads.

He claims his second ballad was sung by a woman who had been turned into a fish because she would not have sex with her boyfriend. She sang it on the 80th of April at 240,000 feet above water!

Make up your own ballad of a similar incredible event.

---

cozened cheated	**a life** on my life
behoves cautions, is wise for	**Five justices' … it** sworn true by
parcels of charge expensive goods	five judges

MOPSA I have done. Come, you promised me a tawdry-lace and a pair
of sweet gloves.

CLOWN Have I not told thee how I was cozened by the way and lost all
my money?   240

AUTOLYCUS And indeed, sir, there are cozeners abroad; therefore it
behoves men to be wary.

CLOWN Fear not thou, man, thou shalt lose nothing here.

AUTOLYCUS I hope so, sir, for I have about me many parcels of charge.

CLOWN What hast here? Ballads?   245

MOPSA Pray now, buy some. I love a ballad in print, a life, for then we
are sure they are true.

AUTOLYCUS Here's one to a very doleful tune, how a usurer's wife was
brought to bed of twenty money-bags at a burden, and how she
longed to eat adders' heads and toads carbonadoed.   250

MOPSA Is it true, think you?

AUTOLYCUS Very true, and but a month old.

DORCAS Bless me from marrying a usurer!

AUTOLYCUS Here's the midwife's name to't, one Mistress Taleporter,
and five or six honest wives that were present. Why should I carry   255
lies abroad?

MOPSA Pray you now, buy it.

CLOWN Come on, lay it by, and let's first see more ballads; we'll buy the
other things anon.

AUTOLYCUS Here's another ballad, of a fish that appeared upon the   260
coast on Wednesday the fourscore of April, forty thousand fathom
above water, and sung this ballad against the hard hearts of maids.
It was thought she was a woman, and was turned into a cold fish
for she would not exchange flesh with one that loved her. The
ballad is very pitiful, and as true.   265

DORCAS Is it true too, think you?

AUTOLYCUS Five justices' hands at it, and witnesses more than my
pack will hold.

CLOWN Lay it by too. Another.

AUTOLYCUS This is a merry ballad, but a very pretty one.   270

MOPSA Let's have some merry ones.

Autolycus, Mopsa and Dorcas sing a ballad in which two maids woo one man. Mopsa and Dorcas are led away by the Clown, who promises to buy gifts for them.

Autolycus, with accordion, leads the singing.
How would you perform the song?

1 'Follow me, girls' (in small groups)

Explore various ways of staging the exit of the Clown, Mopsa and Dorcas. Remember that the Clown may feel that Autolycus is beginning to steal the girls' affections.

passing exceedingly
westward in the west country
bear a part take a part in the song
becomes thy oath suits your promise

have this song out anon sing the ballad soon
sad serious

AUTOLYCUS Why, this is a passing merry one, and goes to the tune of 'Two maids wooing a man'. There's scarce a maid westward but she sings it; 'tis in request, I can tell you.

MOPSA We can both sing it. If thou'lt bear a part, thou shalt hear; 'tis in three parts.   275

DORCAS We had the tune on't a month ago.

AUTOLYCUS I can bear my part: you must know 'tis my occupation. Have at it with you.

[They sing]

AUTOLYCUS	Get you hence, for I must go 280
	Where it fits not you to know.
DORCAS	Whither?
MOPSA	O whither?
DORCAS	Whither?
MOPSA	It becomes thy oath full well
	Thou to me thy secrets tell.
DORCAS	Me too; let me go thither. 285
MOPSA	Or thou goest to the grange or mill.
DORCAS	If to either, thou dost ill.
AUTOLYCUS	Neither.
DORCAS	What, neither?
AUTOLYCUS	Neither.
DORCAS	Thou hast sworn my love to be.
MOPSA	Thou hast sworn it more to me: 290
	Then whither goest? Say, whither?

CLOWN We'll have this song out anon by ourselves; my father and the gentlemen are in sad talk, and we'll not trouble them. Come, bring away thy pack after me. Wenches, I'll buy for you both. Pedlar, let's have the first choice. Follow me, girls.   295

[Exeunt Clown, Dorcas, and Mopsa]

AUTOLYCUS And you shall pay well for 'em.

As he leaves, Autolycus sings an invitation to buy his goods.
A servant announces the arrival of twelve herdsmen who dance
for the assembled company.

1 High-class entertainment?

'Saltiers' is probably a mispronunciation of 'satyrs'. Satyrs were mythological creatures with the upper body and face of a man, but with the ears, budding horns, legs and tail of a goat. Traditionally they were over-sexed. The dance by these 'men of hair' may be the same as that in Ben Jonson's *The Masque of Oberon* performed for King James I on 1st January 1611: 'an antic dance, full of gesture and swift motion'.

The Servant expects to enjoy the Saltiers' dance, even though the 'wenches' have criticised it as a 'gallimaufry of gambols' (a ridiculous mish-mash of leaping about). He shows an awareness of the social class of their visitors as he feels it may be 'too rough' an entertainment for those who know 'little but bowling' (a respectable pastime). The Shepherd dismisses it for the same reason, as 'homely foolery' which will 'weary' the visitors.

But Polixenes welcomes the dance: 'You weary those that refresh us.' How would he say line 314? As a rebuke? Politely? As a sincere compliment? Sarcastically? Or …?

2 A dance for today? (in groups of any size)

If you had chosen to perform your production of *The Winter's Tale* in modern dress, what kind of rustic contemporary dance might you choose? Morris dancing? Line-dancing? Scottish reel? Or …? Make a decision and work out your own lively dance.

Money's … ware-a money is a busybody that spreads goods around
neat-herds cowherds

are o'th'mind believe
by th'square precisely
prating chattering

[He follows them, singing]

Will you buy any tape,
Or lace for your cape,
My dainty duck, my dear-a?
    Any silk, any thread,   300
    Any toys for your head
Of the new'st and fin'st, fin'st wear-a?
    Come to the pedlar,
    Money's a meddler
That doth utter all men's ware-a.   305

                               Exit

[Enter a SERVANT]

SERVANT   Master, there is three carters, three shepherds, three
neat-herds, three swine-herds, that have made themselves all men
of hair; they call themselves Saltiers, and they have a dance which
the wenches say is a gallimaufry of gambols, because they are not
in't; but they themselves are o'th'mind, if it be not too rough for   310
some that know little but bowling, it will please plentifully.
SHEPHERD   Away! We'll none on't; here has been too much homely
foolery already. I know, sir, we weary you.
POLIXENES   You weary those that refresh us. Pray let's see these four
threes of herdsmen.   315
SERVANT   One three of them, by their own report, sir, hath danced
before the king, and not the worst of the three but jumps twelve
foot and a half by th'square.
SHEPHERD   Leave your prating. Since these good men are pleased, let
them come in; but quickly now.   320
SERVANT   Why, they stay at door, sir.

[He lets them in]

Here a dance of twelve SATYRS [*, after which they retire*]

Polixenes thinks it time that Florizel and Perdita are separated.
He asks Florizel why he bought no gifts from Autolycus.
Florizel says his gift to Perdita is love, and promises her life-long love.

1 Director's decisions (in pairs)

a It is some time since Florizel and Perdita have spoken. Decide what they have been doing during Autolycus' appearance and the dance. Their behaviour should not distract the audience from the main action, but should contribute to it.

b Advise the actor playing the part of Polixenes how to deliver line 322. What do you think he means?

c Draw a stage plan showing where your actors would be in relation to one another during lines 322–48.

2 'Love or bounty'

Polixenes remembers that when he was young and in love he showered his lady with gifts (knacks), and he criticises Florizel for not buying Perdita anything from the pedlar. Florizel affirms that the only gifts Perdita values are in his heart: his love. He then launches into a public declaration of his love for Perdita, but is interrupted by the disguised Polixenes.

a How important do you think gifts are in proving love?

b Why does Polixenes interrupt at line 344? And how do Florizel and Perdita react to the interruption?

---

simple innocent, foolish
Sooth in truth
handed love had a love affair
was wont/To used to
nothing marted with bought nothing from

Interpretation should abuse should misinterpret
were straited/For would find it hard to give
breathe my life make a life-long promise
bolted sifted (like flour)

POLIXENES [*To Shepherd*] O, father, you'll know more of that
    hereafter.
    [*To Camillo*] Is it not too far gone? 'Tis time to part them.
    He's simple and tells much. [*To Florizel*] How now, fair
    shepherd!
    Your heart is full of something that does take   325
    Your mind from feasting. Sooth, when I was young
    And handed love as you do I was wont
    To load my she with knacks. I would have ransacked
    The pedlar's silken treasury and have poured it
    To her acceptance. You have let him go   330
    And nothing marted with him. If your lass
    Interpretation should abuse and call this
    Your lack of love or bounty, you were straited
    For a reply, at least if you make a care
    Of happy holding her.
FLORIZEL   Old sir, I know   335
    She prizes not such trifles as these are.
    The gifts she looks from me are packed and locked
    Up in my heart, which I have given already,
    But not delivered. [*To Perdita*] O, hear me breathe my life
    Before this ancient sir, whom, it should seem,   340
    Hath sometime loved. I take thy hand, this hand,
    As soft as dove's down and as white as it,
    Or Ethiopian's tooth, or the fanned snow that's bolted
    By th'northern blasts twice o'er.
POLIXENES   What follows this?
    How prettily th'young swain seems to wash   345
    The hand was fair before! I have put you out;
    But to your protestation: let me hear
    What you profess.

Florizel asks Polixenes and Camillo, and the whole world, to witness his commitment to Perdita. She says she has equal love for him. Florizel asks the Shepherd to declare their betrothal.

---

1 Dramatic irony (in small groups)

Dramatic irony heightens the tension, because Florizel's sincere declaration of his love for Perdita is made in the presence of his disguised father.

Florizel is quite unaware that when he says at line 366 'One being dead' (a reference to his father), his father is present.

Take parts as Florizel, Perdita, Polixenes, Camillo and the Shepherd, and speak the lines opposite. Then repeat your reading, but insert pauses for Polixenes to give his thoughts on all that is said. Discuss how this exercise heightens your awareness of the dramatic irony.

2 Now or future?

In Shakespeare's day there were two different kinds of contracts to marry. One was the equivalent of a public engagement to marry in the future: *per verba de futuro*. This betrothal could be broken if circumstances changed. There was also *per verba de praesenti*, which was again a public declaration but this constituted a legally binding marriage.

What kind of commitment do you think Florizel intends when he says: 'But come on,/Contract us 'fore these witnesses.'?

3 Shared lines (in groups of five)

Every speech opposite begins with a shared line. Some actors say that when a line is shared, there should be no pause between speakers. Do you agree? Experiment with different ways of speaking the opposite page (with and without pauses) to arrive at your decision. See also pages 138 and 215.

---

perdition loss
By th'pattern ... of his my own
  feelings are an exact image of his

Her portion Perdita's dowry
Enough time enough

FLORIZEL   Do, and be witness to't.
POLIXENES And this my neighbour too?
FLORIZEL   And he, and more
    Than he, and men – the earth, the heavens, and all: 350
    That were I crowned the most imperial monarch,
    Thereof most worthy, were I the fairest youth
    That ever made eye swerve, had force and knowledge
    More than was ever man's, I would not prize them
    Without her love; for her employ them all,   355
    Commend them and condemn them to her service
    Or to their own perdition.
POLIXENES   Fairly offered.
CAMILLO This shows a sound affection.
SHEPHERD   But, my daughter,
    Say you the like to him?
PERDITA   I cannot speak
    So well, nothing so well; no, nor mean better.   360
    By th'pattern of mine own thoughts I cut out
    The purity of his.
SHEPHERD   Take hands, a bargain!
    And, friends unknown, you shall bear witness to't.
    I give my daughter to him, and will make
    Her portion equal his.
FLORIZEL   O, that must be   365
    I'th'virtue of your daughter. One being dead,
    I shall have more than you can dream of yet;
    Enough then for your wonder. But come on,
    Contract us 'fore these witnesses.

*Polixenes argues strongly that Florizel's father should be at the wedding.
Florizel rejects the suggestion, saying that he has good reasons.
He demands that the wedding proceed.*

1 Act it out (in groups of five)

Lines 369–96 are full of different dramatic tensions. Almost every
speech begins with a shared line of verse, suggesting that all the cues
are taken up very quickly (see pages 136 and 215). Polixenes wishes to
make Florizel admit that his father should be present at the wedding,
but Florizel refuses. Try the following ways of rehearsing the script,
taking parts as Florizel, Polixenes, the Shepherd, Perdita and Camillo.

- Speak the lines first with short pauses between each speaker, and
  then with no pause.
- Speak with the cast in different 'blockings' (different physical
  positions), for example, with Perdita and Florizel together, or
  separated by the Shepherd, or Polixenes. Where is Camillo? Can
  you agree on a preferred way of 'blocking'?
- Think about the atmosphere of this episode (funny? touching?
  frightening? or …?). Experiment with different tones of voice to
  find a mood you feel is appropriate.
- Mime the episode, with Perdita speaking a narration which is her
  own version of each speech.
- Neither Perdita nor Camillo speak. How should they behave?

Soft easy now, wait!
best becomes the table is most
  suitable at the feast
alt'ring rheums moodiness, ill-
  humours
dispute his own estate manage
  his own finances

being childish when he was a child
Something unfilial which a son
  should not do
all whose joy … posterity whose
  chief delight is fine grandchildren

SHEPHERD   Come, your hand;
          And, daughter, yours.
POLIXENES   Soft, swain, awhile, beseech you.   370
          Have you a father?
FLORIZEL   I have; but what of him?
POLIXENES Knows he of this?
FLORIZEL   He neither does nor shall.
POLIXENES Methinks a father
          Is at the nuptial of his son a guest
          That best becomes the table. Pray you once more,   375
          Is not your father grown incapable
          Of reasonable affairs? Is he not stupid
          With age and alt'ring rheums? Can he speak, hear,
          Know man from man, dispute his own estate?
          Lies he not bed-rid, and again does nothing   380
          But what he did being childish?
FLORIZEL   No, good sir;
          He has his health, and ampler strength indeed
          Than most have of his age.
POLIXENES   By my white beard,
          You offer him, if this be so, a wrong
          Something unfilial. Reason my son   385
          Should choose himself a wife, but as good reason
          The father, all whose joy is nothing else
          But fair posterity, should hold some counsel
          In such a business.
FLORIZEL   I yield all this;
          But for some other reasons, my grave sir,   390
          Which 'tis not fit you know, I not acquaint
          My father of this business.
POLIXENES   Let him know't.
FLORIZEL He shall not.
POLIXENES   Prithee, let him.
FLORIZEL   No, he must not.
SHEPHERD Let him, my son. He shall not need to grieve
          At knowing of thy choice.
FLORIZEL   Come, come, he must not.   395
          Mark our contract.

Polixenes reveals his identity and orders Florizel to give up Perdita or lose his title. He lifts his death sentence on the Shepherd, but threatens Perdita with death and torture if she ever sees Florizel again.

---

1 Revealed

Decide how Polixenes can remove his disguise without being melodramatic and provoking an unwanted laugh from the audience.

2 Polixenes' threats (in groups of four)

a Speak Polixenes' lines 396–420, changing speaker at each punctuation mark. Talk about how Shakespeare conveys Polixenes' mood through syntax and punctuation.

b List the words and phrases Polixenes uses to describe Perdita. Make a similar list of the ways he describes his son. Use your lists to work out the motives for Polixenes' anger. How much is it to do with social class?

c Polixenes' lines contain many references to people. An exercise called deixis (pointing) can help to make the meaning clearer. Take parts as Polixenes, the Shepherd, Florizel and Perdita. As one person slowly speaks Polixenes' lines, everyone points to each character as they are mentioned in some way (for example, the first naming of Perdita is as 'sheep-hook').

d Write a modern speech, in blank verse if you can, from a father to a son who has displeased him. Try to copy the way that Shakespeare uses punctuation and word order to direct the actor.

---

sceptre's heir heir to the throne
affects a sheep-hook takes up
  with a shepherd's crook (Perdita)
cop'st with have to do with
homely plain
state position, status

knack worthless girl
Farre than Deucalion off further
  distant from me than Deucalion
  (Greek equivalent of Noah)
churl villain
latches gates

POLIXENES [*Removing his disguise*] Mark your divorce, young sir,
   Whom son I dare not call: thou art too base
   To be acknowledged. Thou a sceptre's heir,
   That thus affects a sheep-hook! [*To the Shepherd*] Thou, old traitor,
   I am sorry that by hanging thee I can   400
   But shorten thy life one week. [*To Perdita*] And thou, fresh piece
   Of excellent witchcraft, who of force must know
   The royal fool thou cop'st with –
SHEPHERD   O, my heart!
POLIXENES I'll have thy beauty scratched with briars and made
   More homely than thy state. For thee, fond boy,   405
   If I may ever know thou dost but sigh
   That thou no more shalt never see this knack – as never
   I mean thou shalt – we'll bar thee from succession,
   Not hold thee of our blood, no, not our kin,
   Farre than Deucalion off. Mark thou my words.   410
   Follow us to the court. Thou, churl, for this time,
   Though full of our displeasure, yet we free thee
   From the dead blow of it. And you, enchantment,
   Worthy enough a herdsman – yea, him too
   That makes himself, but for our honour therein,   415
   Unworthy thee – if ever henceforth thou
   These rural latches to his entrance open,
   Or hoop his body more with thy embraces,
   I will devise a death as cruel for thee
   As thou art tender to't.   *Exit*

Perdita says that she was not afraid, but urges Florizel to leave.
The Shepherd reproaches Florizel and Perdita for their actions.
Camillo advises Florizel to avoid Polixenes while his temper rages.

1 Everyone's equal

Perdita almost told Polixenes that everyone lives under the same sun. Since she says she was not much afraid of Polixenes, why did she not speak her egalitarian thoughts?

2 'Why look you so upon me?'

What is Perdita's facial expression at line 441? What is she thinking?

3 The Shepherd's despair

In lines 436–7, the Shepherd (who is eighty-three years old) imagines his execution and burial, having forgotten that Polixenes has reprieved him. Hanged people were buried at the foot of the gallows without a funeral service.

Every actor who plays the Shepherd has to decide whether or not he wishes to make the audience laugh during his single speech opposite. What would you do? Step into role and speak all the Shepherd's lines, first for comic, then for tragic effect. Which do you prefer?

4 'You know your father's temper'

Polixenes seems well-known at court for his bad moods (line 446). But might Camillo be talking less about Polixenes' anger than his willingness to forgive after his fury has subsided? Which seems more likely to you?

Beseech you I implore you
mingle faith join in a pledge of
  marriage

More straining ... unwillingly
  even more eager to go on (with
  marriage) now I am being pulled
  back

PERDITA   Even here undone!   420
I was not much afeard, for once or twice
I was about to speak and tell him plainly
The self-same sun that shines upon his court
Hides not his visage from our cottage but
Looks on alike. [*To Florizel*] Will't please you, sir, be gone?   425
I told you what would come of this. Beseech you
Of your own state take care. This dream of mine
Being now awake, I'll queen it no inch farther,
But milk my ewes, and weep.

CAMILLO   Why, how now, father!
Speak ere thou diest.

SHEPHERD   I cannot speak, nor think,   430
Nor dare to know that which I know. [*To Florizel*] O sir,
You have undone a man of fourscore three
That thought to fill his grave in quiet, yea,
To die upon the bed my father died,
To lie close by his honest bones. But now   435
Some hangman must put on my shroud and lay me
Where no priest shovels in dust. [*To Perdita*] O cursèd
wretch,
That knew'st this was the prince, and wouldst adventure
To mingle faith with him! Undone, undone!
If I might die within this hour, I have lived   440
To die when I desire.   *Exit*

FLORIZEL   Why look you so upon me?
I am but sorry, not afeard; delayed,
But nothing altered. What I was, I am;
More straining on for plucking back, not following
My leash unwillingly.

CAMILLO   Gracious my lord,   445
You know your father's temper. At this time
He will allow no speech – which I do guess
You do not purpose to him – and as hardly
Will he endure your sight as yet, I fear.
Then, till the fury of his highness settle,   450
Come not before him.

Camillo removes his disguise. Florizel rejects his title to the crown, and makes a firm statement of his commitment to Perdita. He says they will flee the country on his ship.

1 Disguise

Florizel guesses he is speaking to Camillo. Stage conventions often mean that all disguises, however meagre, are effective. In *Twelfth Night* Viola, dressed as a boy, is taken for her twin brother. In *As You Like It* even the man who loves her does not recognise the disguised Rosalind. In the costume inventory of the Elizabethan theatre owner Philip Henslowe, there was 'a cloake to go invisible'. What kind of disguise do you think would be suitable for Camillo, and what might he do at 'Even he, my lord' (line 452) to reveal his identity to Florizel?

2 Florizel's imagery (in pairs)

In lines 457–8, Shakespeare uses an image of the earth's destruction. He used a similar image in *Macbeth* ('though the treasure/Of nature's germen tumble altogether,/Even till destruction sicken'), and in *King Lear* ('Strike flat the thick rotundity o'th'world'). Turn to page 214 and read the section on imagery, then identify other images Florizel uses on the facing page. Talk together about how vivid you find them.

3 An emphatic vow

Florizel is determined to obey what his emotions tell him. He vows that he will not give up his promise to Perdita, literally for the world. Speak his vow in lines 467–71 as emphatically as you can, by stressing the rhythm, his use of repetition and all the verbs.

---

violation of my faith breaking of my vow
fancy love
I have reason I remain sane
thereat gleaned found there (as in harvest)

wombs holds within it
cast ... passion give your good advice to calm his temper
Tug fight it out
design purpose

FLORIZEL   I not purpose it.
    I think, Camillo?
CAMILLO   Even he, my lord.
PERDITA How often have I told you 'twould be thus!
    How often said my dignity would last
    But till 'twere known!
FLORIZEL   It cannot fail but by   455
    The violation of my faith; and then
    Let nature crush the sides o'th'earth together
    And mar the seeds within! Lift up thy looks.
    From my succession wipe me, father; I
    Am heir to my affection.
CAMILLO   Be advised.   460
FLORIZEL I am, and by my fancy. If my reason
    Will thereto be obedient, I have reason;
    If not, my senses, better pleased with madness,
    Do bid it welcome.
CAMILLO   This is desperate, sir.
FLORIZEL So call it; but it does fulfil my vow: 465
    I needs must think it honesty. Camillo,
    Not for Bohemia, nor the pomp that may
    Be thereat gleaned, for all the sun sees, or
    The close earth wombs, or the profound seas hides
    In unknown fathoms, will I break my oath   470
    To this my fair beloved. Therefore, I pray you,
    As you have ever been my father's honoured friend,
    When he shall miss me – as, in faith, I mean not
    To see him any more – cast your good counsels
    Upon his passion. Let myself and fortune   475
    Tug for the time to come. This you may know,
    And so deliver: I am put to sea
    With her who here I cannot hold on shore;
    And, most opportune to our need, I have
    A vessel rides fast by, but not prepared   480
    For this design. What course I mean to hold
    Shall nothing benefit your knowledge nor
    Concern me the reporting.
CAMILLO   O my lord,
    I would your spirit were easier for advice,
    Or stronger for your need.

*Camillo wishes to use Florizel's predicament to assist his own return to
Sicilia, where he longs to see Leontes. He offers to help Florizel marry
Perdita and be reconciled with Polixenes.*

1 Camillo's soliloquy (in pairs)

Camillo's lines 486–92 are a soliloquy or long aside, in which, unheard
by the others on stage, he reveals his true thoughts to the audience. He
shows he has a double objective: to save Florizel, and to return to
Sicilia.

a Would you advise Camillo to speak the lines to himself or direct
  to the audience?

b What could Florizel and Perdita be doing as Camillo speaks?
  They are on stage, but are supposed to be unable to overhear him.
  Devise a short exchange for Florizel and Perdita to speak during
  Camillo's aside to maintain their concentration on their roles.

2 The qualities of a confidante (in pairs)

What kind of person is Camillo? He had been promoted by Leontes to
be his closest adviser. He now seems to occupy the same role in
Polixenes' court. Brainstorm a list of words that you feel are the
essential qualities of a confidante (someone entrusted with secrets).
When you have a list of at least ten, check how many you feel describe
Camillo.

3 Flattering words

Camillo wants to ensure that Florizel accepts his plan, so he chooses his
words carefully between lines 494–512. Pick out one or two words in
each line that you think might have special appeal to Florizel. Then
practise speaking the lines – perhaps stressing those words to achieve
an appropriate tone.

---

irremoveable immovable
frame use
fraught preoccupied
curious worrying
as thought on as soon as they are
  thought of
direction plan, instruction

ponderous and settled important
  and definite
disjunction separation
forfend forbid
discontenting angry
qualify calm, pacify
up to liking to love you again

FLORIZEL   Hark, Perdita –   485
    [To Camillo] I'll hear you by and by.

        [He draws Perdita aside]

CAMILLO   He's irremoveable,
    Resolved for flight. Now were I happy if
    His going I could frame to serve my turn,
    Save him from danger, do him love and honour,
    Purchase the sight again of dear Sicilia   490
    And that unhappy king, my master, whom
    I so much thirst to see.
FLORIZEL   Now, good Camillo,
    I am so fraught with curious business that
    I leave out ceremony.
CAMILLO   Sir, I think
    You have heard of my poor services i'th'love   495
    That I have borne your father?
FLORIZEL   Very nobly
    Have you deserved. It is my father's music
    To speak your deeds, not little of his care
    To have them recompensed as thought on.
CAMILLO   Well, my lord,
    If you may please to think I love the king,   500
    And through him what's nearest to him, which is
    Your gracious self, embrace but my direction,
    If your more ponderous and settled project
    May suffer alteration. On mine honour,
    I'll point you where you shall have such receiving   505
    As shall become your highness; where you may
    Enjoy your mistress, from the whom I see
    There's no disjunction to be made but by –
    As heavens forfend – your ruin; marry her;
    And, with my best endeavours in your absence,   510
    Your discontenting father strive to qualify,
    And bring him up to liking.

*Florizel says he has no clear plan, but will risk whatever comes.
Camillo explains his plan for Florizel and Perdita to visit Leontes as
Polixenes' envoys. They are likely to find a warm welcome.*

1 'The slaves of chance' (in small groups)

Shakespeare often raises the question of destiny. In *King Lear*, Gloucester says that humans have no control over their destiny, 'As flies to wanton boys are we to the gods. They kill us for their sport.' But in *Julius Caesar*, Brutus argues that human beings can determine their own fortune, 'There is a tide in the affairs of men which taken at the flood leads on to fortune.'

In lines 517–20, Florizel seems to believe in chance more than destiny. Talk about the degree of control you feel you have over your life, how far you feel it is controlled by external forces and how far by chance.

A fourteenth-century Wheel of Fortune. How might it illustrate Florizel's mind in lines 517–20?

2 Camillo's plan
(in groups of four)

In lines 520–43, Camillo explains his plans for going to Sicilia. Speak his lines, then give your responses to the each of the following:

a Are Camillo's motives selfish?

b Perdita is not part of the discussion. Why not?

c What do you think will happen in Sicilia? Check your prediction when you reach Act 5.

d Suggest several things Camillo intends to write down (line 539).

guilty/To to blame for	**point you ... sitting** guide you on
list listen	every occasion
habited dressed	**bosom** personal confidence
free arms arms freely	**sap** wisdom, hopeful prospect
colour reason	

FLORIZEL   How, Camillo,
    May this, almost a miracle, be done?
    That I may call thee something more than man,
    And after that trust to thee.
CAMILLO   Have you thought on   515
    A place whereto you'll go?
FLORIZEL   Not any yet;
    But as th'unthought-on accident is guilty
    To what we wildly do, so we profess
    Ourselves to be the slaves of chance and flies
    Of every wind that blows.
CAMILLO   Then list to me.   520
    This follows, if you will not change your purpose
    But undergo this flight: make for Sicilia,
    And there present yourself and your fair princess –
    For so I see she must be – 'fore Leontes.
    She shall be habited as it becomes   525
    The partner of your bed. Methinks I see
    Leontes opening his free arms and weeping
    His welcomes forth; asks thee, the son, forgiveness,
    As 'twere i'th'father's person; kisses the hands
    Of your fresh princess; o'er and o'er divides him   530
    'Twixt his unkindness and his kindness: th'one
    He chides to hell, and bids the other grow
    Faster than thought or time.
FLORIZEL   Worthy Camillo,
    What colour for my visitation shall I
    Hold up before him?
CAMILLO   Sent by the king your father   535
    To greet him and to give him comforts. Sir,
    The manner of your bearing towards him, with
    What you, as from your father, shall deliver –
    Things known betwixt us three – I'll write you down,
    The which shall point you forth at every sitting   540
    What you must say, that he shall not perceive
    But that you have your father's bosom there
    And speak his very heart.
FLORIZEL   I am bound to you;
    There is some sap in this.

Camillo argues that his scheme is better than Florizel's unplanned flight, and that success will strengthen love. Camillo and Florizel praise the steadfast love and courage of Perdita.

1 Love: unaltered by 'affliction'? (in pairs)

Camillo says that love is changed by adversity (lines 551–4). Perdita disagrees: troubles can affect your appearance ('affliction may subdue the cheek'), but not your love for someone. Shakespeare offers a similar view to Perdita in Sonnet 116:

Let me not to the marriage of true minds
Admit impediments; love is not love
Which alters when it alteration finds,
Or bends with the remover to remove.
O no, it is an ever-fixèd mark
That looks on tempests and is never shaken;
It is the star to every wand'ring bark,
Whose worth's unknown, although his heighth be taken.
Love's not Time's fool, though rosy lips and cheeks
Within his bending sickle's compass come;
Love alters not with his brief hours and weeks,
But bears it out even to the edge of doom.
If this be error and upon me proved,
I never writ, nor no man ever loved.

Use Camillo's and Perdita's lines, and Sonnet 116 to discuss the different views of Camillo and Perdita. Do external circumstances alter love?

2 Praising Perdita

In lines 558–60, Florizel says Perdita's behaviour is far beyond that expected from someone of low status ('i'th'rear our birth'); Camillo says she can teach high-status people good behaviour. Do the two men's views sound snobbish or sincere to you? Or …?

---

wild dedication rash adventure
loath unwilling
Prosperity good fortune
Affliction alters misfortune changes for the worse

subdue the cheek change the appearance
furnished dressed
royally appointed dressed like a prince
instance example

CAMILLO   A course more promising
　　　Than a wild dedication of yourselves   545
　　　To unpathed waters, undreamed shores, most certain
　　　To miseries enough; no hope to help you,
　　　But as you shake off one to take another;
　　　Nothing so certain as your anchors, who
　　　Do their best office if they can but stay you   550
　　　Where you'll be loath to be. Besides, you know
　　　Prosperity's the very bond of love,
　　　Whose fresh complexion and whose heart together
　　　Affliction alters.
PERDITA   One of these is true:
　　　I think affliction may subdue the cheek,   555
　　　But not take in the mind.
CAMILLO   Yea, say you so?
　　　There shall not at your father's house these seven years
　　　Be born another such.
FLORIZEL   My good Camillo,
　　　She's as forward of her breeding as
　　　She is i'th'rear our birth.
CAMILLO   I cannot say 'tis pity   560
　　　She lacks instructions, for she seems a mistress
　　　To most that teach.
PERDITA   Your pardon, sir; for this
　　　I'll blush you thanks.
FLORIZEL   My prettiest Perdita!
　　　But O, the thorns we stand upon! Camillo –
　　　Preserver of my father, now of me,   565
　　　The medicine of our house – how shall we do?
　　　We are not furnished like Bohemia's son,
　　　Nor shall appear in Sicilia.
CAMILLO   My lord,
　　　Fear none of this. I think you know my fortunes
　　　Do all lie there. It shall be so my care   570
　　　To have you royally appointed as if
　　　The scene you play were mine. For instance, sir,
　　　That you may know you shall not want, one word.

[They talk apart]

Autolycus relates his success in selling all his stock and cheating the country people. Camillo decides to use Autolycus in the escape plan. He pays Autolycus to change clothes with Florizel.

1 Cheating and thieving (in small groups)

Autolycus has sold all his 'trumpery': showy but worthless items. Not one imitation jewel ('counterfeit stone'), perfume case ('pomander'), or notebook ('table-book') remains. The shepherds and shepherdesses had clustered around him, eager to buy, making it easy for him to steal their purses. Speak Autolycus' lines, then choose one of the following:

a A 'horn-ring' was thought to have magic properties. Step into role as a descendant of Autolycus presenting a TV advertisement for this product, and sell it to the rest of the group.

b You are a street market trader. Using modern equivalents for the contents of Autolycus' pack, sell your wares.

c Improvise the action that Autolycus describes. Make it as lively and entertaining as you can.

2 Design Autolycus' costume

Camillo orders Autolycus and Florizel to change clothes, and says that Autolycus will come off better from the exchange. But Florizel is dressed as a shepherd ('obscured with a swain's wearing', line 9). So what is Autolycus wearing?

---

fasting starving
benediction blessing
best in picture most worth stealing
pettitoes trotters
all their other ... ears they saw nothing

geld ... purse cut the purse from a man's belt
whoobub hubbub
choughs foolish birds
discase undress
pennyworth bargain
boot compensation, reward

Enter AUTOLYCUS

AUTOLYCUS   Ha, ha, what a fool Honesty is! And Trust, his sworn
brother, a very simple gentleman! I have sold all my trumpery – not   575
a counterfeit stone, not a ribbon, glass, pomander, brooch,
table-book, ballad, knife, tape, glove, shoe-tie, bracelet, horn-ring,
to keep my pack from fasting. They throng who should buy first,
as if my trinkets had been hallowed and brought a benediction to
the buyer; by which means I saw whose purse was best in picture,   580
and what I saw to my good use I remembered. My clown, who
wants but something to be a reasonable man, grew so in love with
the wenches' song that he would not stir his pettitoes till he had
both tune and words, which so drew the rest of the herd to me that
all their other senses stuck in ears. You might have pinched a   585
placket, it was senseless; 'twas nothing to geld a codpiece of a purse;
I would have filed keys off that hung in chains. No hearing, no
feeling, but my sir's song, and admiring the nothing of it. So that
in this time of lethargy I picked and cut most of their festival
purses, and had not the old man come in with a whoobub against   590
his daughter and the king's son and scared my choughs from the
chaff, I had not left a purse alive in the whole army.
        [*Camillo, Florizel, and Perdita come forward*]
CAMILLO   Nay, but my letters, by this means being there
        So soon as you arrive, shall clear that doubt.
FLORIZEL   And those that you'll procure from King Leontes?   595
CAMILLO   Shall satisfy your father.
PERDITA   Happy be you!
        All that you speak shows fair.
CAMILLO   [*Seeing Autolycus*]   Who have we here?
        We'll make an instrument of this, omit
        Nothing may give us aid.
AUTOLYCUS   [*Aside*] If they have overheard me now, why, hanging.   600
CAMILLO   How now, good fellow! Why shak'st thou so? Fear not, man;
        here's no harm intended to thee.
AUTOLYCUS   I am a poor fellow, sir.
CAMILLO   Why, be so still, here's nobody will steal that from thee. Yet
        for the outside of thy poverty we must make an exchange; therefore   605
        discase thee instantly – thou must think there's a necessity in't –
        and change garments with this gentleman. Though the pennyworth
        on his side be the worst, yet hold thee, [*Giving him money*] there's
        some boot.

Florizel and Autolycus exchange clothes. Camillo decides to tell Polixenes of the flight of the lovers so that the king will follow them to Sicilia with Camillo.

1 Changing clothes (in pairs)

Actors undressing and dressing on stage invent all kinds of actions. One production had Florizel and Autolycus behind different trees throwing garments to each other. Sometimes they missed and had to run out, half dressed, to retrieve the items of clothing. In another production, Autolycus addressed both his asides to Florizel's shirt and breeches. All Perdita seems to have offered to her is a hat, though Camillo gives her much advice. She should go behind a bush ('retire yourself/Into some covert') to remove some outer clothing ('Dismantle') and disguise her appearance ('disliken the truth/Of your own seeming').

Work out how you would stage lines 610–16, and suggest how Perdita might disguise herself.

2 *'They talk apart'* (in pairs)

The stage direction at line 630 is a device to allow Camillo a short soliloquy [*Aside*] to let the audience know his plans. Invent some stage business for Florizel and Perdita that is dramatically convincing (just what is it that they have both 'forgot' at line 629?).

3 'A woman's longing' (in pairs)

In line 636, Camillo describes his extremely strong desire to return to Sicilia as 'a woman's longing'. Give your response to his image (is a woman's longing more powerful than a man's?).

---

dispatch hurry
flayed undressed
smell the trick on't suspect some
  trickery here

earnest (line 614) money as a bribe
eyes over spies
undescried undetected
twain two

AUTOLYCUS I am a poor fellow, sir. [*Aside*] I know ye well enough.   610
CAMILLO Nay, prithee dispatch; the gentleman is half flayed already.
AUTOLYCUS Are you in earnest, sir? [*Aside*] I smell the trick on't.
FLORIZEL Dispatch, I prithee.
AUTOLYCUS Indeed, I have had earnest, but I cannot with conscience
    take it.   615
CAMILLO Unbuckle, unbuckle.

      [*Florizel and Autolycus exchange garments*]

      Fortunate mistress – let my prophecy
      Come home to ye! – you must retire yourself
      Into some covert, take your sweetheart's hat
      And pluck it o'er your brows, muffle your face,   620
      Dismantle you, and, as you can, disliken
      The truth of your own seeming, that you may –
      For I do fear eyes over – to shipboard
      Get undescried.
PERDITA   I see the play so lies
      That I must bear a part.
CAMILLO   No remedy.   625
      Have you done there?
FLORIZEL   Should I now meet my father,
      He would not call me son.
CAMILLO   Nay, you shall have no hat.

      [*He gives the hat to Perdita*]

      Come, lady, come. Farewell, my friend.
AUTOLYCUS   Adieu, sir.
FLORIZEL O Perdita, what have we twain forgot!
      Pray you, a word.   630

         [*They talk apart*]

CAMILLO [*Aside*] What I do next shall be to tell the king
      Of this escape and whither they are bound;
      Wherein my hope is I shall so prevail
      To force him after, in whose company
      I shall re-view Sicilia, for whose sight   635
      I have a woman's longing.

Autolycus says that he has grasped the plot, but resolves not to reveal it to King Polixenes. He hides to overhear the Shepherd and Clown discuss their plan to tell the king that Perdita is a foundling.

1 True to character

Because Autolycus thinks that Florizel is engaged in wrongdoing, he decides not to tell the king. To reveal the plot would be the action of an honest man, and Autolycus wishes to remain 'constant to my profession' (consistent in his villainy). Speak his soliloquy, lines 639–49, to bring out his enjoyment of his own knavery.

Which line (from page 159) do you think is being spoken here?

---

boot reward

connive at turn a blind or tolerant eye to

extempore on the spur of the moment

clog Perdita (wooden block tied to the heel of an animal)

session meeting of a law court

changeling baby left by a fairy in exchange for a human child

go whistle go hang itself

I warrant you I assure you

FLORIZEL   Fortune speed us!
  Thus we set on, Camillo, to th'sea-side.
CAMILLO The swifter speed the better.
               Exeunt [Florizel, Perdita, and Camillo]
AUTOLYCUS I understand the business, I hear it. To have an open ear,
  a quick eye, and a nimble hand, is necessary for a cut-purse; a   640
  good nose is requisite also, to smell out work for th'other senses.
  I see this is the time that the unjust man doth thrive. What an
  exchange had this been without boot! What a boot is here with this
  exchange! Sure, the gods do this year connive at us, and we may
  do anything extempore. The prince himself is about a piece of   645
  iniquity – stealing away from his father with his clog at his heels.
  If I thought it were a piece of honesty to acquaint the king withal,
  I would not do't. I hold it the more knavery to conceal it; and
  therein am I constant to my profession.

       [Enter CLOWN *and* SHEPHERD*]*

  Aside, aside! Here is more matter for a hot brain. Every land's end,   650
  every shop, church, session, hanging, yields a careful man work.
CLOWN See, see, what a man you are now! There is no other way but to
  tell the king she's a changeling and none of your flesh and blood.
SHEPHERD Nay, but hear me.
CLOWN Nay, but hear me.   655
SHEPHERD Go to, then.
CLOWN She being none of your flesh and blood, your flesh and blood
  has not offended the king, and so your flesh and blood is not to be
  punished by him. Show those things you found about her – those
  secret things, all but what she has with her. This being done, let   660
  the law go whistle, I warrant you.
SHEPHERD I will tell the king all, every word – yea, and his son's pranks
  too; who, I may say, is no honest man, neither to his father nor to
  me, to go about to make me the king's brother-in-law.
CLOWN Indeed, brother-in-law was the farthest off you could have   665
  been to him, and then your blood had been the dearer by I know
  not how much an ounce.
AUTOLYCUS *[Aside]* Very wisely, puppies!

Autolycus removes his disguise and challenges the Shepherd and his son to tell him where they are going. Autolycus pretends to be a courtier and says he can help or hinder their business with Polixenes.

1 Florizel's clothes (in pairs)

At line 9, Florizel was described by Perdita as being 'obscured with a swain's wearing', and he said to Camillo that he is 'not furnished like Bohemia's son' (line 567). Yet Autolycus is wearing the clothes discarded by Florizel and the Shepherd says 'his garments are rich' (line 707). Talk together about the apparent discrepancy, and how you would manage this if you were in charge of the costumes for a production. One production gave Florizel a large sleeveless jerkin which he wore over his rich apparel.

2 Act it out! (in groups of three)

The whole episode between Autolycus and the two rustics (lines 676–771) offers excellent opportunities for acting out. Autolycus has some knowledge of the court from his days in Florizel's service, and will enjoy parodying a courtier. Take parts and act the episode, with Autolycus using the haughtiest manner he can. Decide who Autolycus addresses at line 703: the audience? imaginary friends? or …?

3 A bird to bribe the judge

The Clown knows only local courts, where it was the custom to bribe officials with gifts of poultry. He thinks that Autolycus is suggesting such a bribe, believing 'advocate' means a pheasant (line 700). Shakespeare refers to the bribes in Jaques' 'Seven Ages of Man' speech in *As You Like It* (Act 2 Scene 7):

'And then the Justice,
In fair round belly, with good capon lined' (bribed with a chicken)

---

fardel bundle	**measure** graceful movement
impediment stumbling block	(as in a dance)
excrement facial hair	**insinuate** cajole
having property	**toaze** tease out, draw out
discover disclose	**cap-à-pie** from head to toe
enfoldings clothes	

SHEPHERD Well, let us to the king. There is that in this fardel will make him scratch his beard. 670

AUTOLYCUS [*Aside*] I know not what impediment this complaint may be to the flight of my master.

CLOWN Pray heartily he be at palace.

AUTOLYCUS [*Aside*] Though I am not naturally honest, I am so sometimes by chance. Let me pocket up my pedlar's excrement. 675

[*He takes off his false beard*]

How now, rustics! Whither are you bound?

SHEPHERD To th'palace, and it like your worship.

AUTOLYCUS Your affairs there, what, with whom, the condition of that fardel, the place of your dwelling, your names, your ages, of what having, breeding, and anything that is fitting to be known, discover. 680

CLOWN We are but plain fellows, sir.

AUTOLYCUS A lie; you are rough and hairy. Let me have no lying, it becomes none but tradesmen, and they often give us soldiers the lie; but we pay them for it with stamped coin, not stabbing steel; therefore they do not give us the lie. 685

CLOWN Your worship had like to have given us one, if you had not taken yourself with the manner.

SHEPHERD Are you a courtier, an't like you, sir?

AUTOLYCUS Whether it like me or no, I am a courtier. Seest thou not the air of the court in these enfoldings? Hath not my gait in it the 690 measure of the court? Receives not thy nose court-odour from me? Reflect I not on thy baseness court-contempt? Think'st thou for that I insinuate or toaze from thee thy business I am therefore no courtier? I am courtier cap-à-pie; and one that will either push on or pluck back thy business there; whereupon I command thee 695 to open thy affair.

SHEPHERD My business, sir, is to the king.

AUTOLYCUS What advocate hast thou to him?

SHEPHERD I know not, an't like you.

CLOWN [*Aside to Shepherd*] Advocate's the court-word for a pheasant. 700 Say you have none.

SHEPHERD None, sir; I have no pheasant, cock nor hen.

AUTOLYCUS How blest are we that are not simple men!
Yet nature might have made me as these are;
Therefore I'll not disdain. 705

CLOWN [*Aside to Shepherd*] This cannot be but a great courtier.

SHEPHERD His garments are rich, but he wears them not handsomely.

Autolycus says Polixenes has embarked on a voyage.
He describes the awful tortures in store for the Shepherd and his son.
He offers to help them by taking them to the king.

1 Help for actors (in groups of three)

The following can help your acting out of this whole episode (see
Activity 2 on page 158).

- 'picking on's teeth' (line 709). Toothpicks were used by upper-
  class travellers, so seeing someone picking their teeth in public
  would seem strange to the country community. Just how is
  Autolycus doing his tooth-picking?

- Tortures (lines 721–40). Autolycus can now indulge his acting
  ability even more as he describes, perhaps with mimed
  accompaniments, the horrific tortures which the Shepherd and his
  son may have to endure. Stoning to death would be the lightest
  punishment! The two proposed victims will be feeling real fear.
  For actors who enjoy going over the top this is the perfect
  humorous episode.

- 'to purge melancholy' (line 717). See page 71 to remind yourself
  of Elizabethan beliefs about humours.

2 Class matters

'Draw our throne into a sheep-cote?' (shepherd's cottage). Autolycus'
sneering comment in line 731 about a prince marrying a shepherd's
daughter reflects what many Jacobeans thought about class structure.
(But the dramatic irony is that Perdita is actually a princess.) Today
many people regard Autolycus' sneer as prejudiced snobbery. What is
your own reaction to his words?

---

fantastical outrageous	**'nointed** covered, anointed
in handfast under arrest	**dram** little bit
wit ingenuity	**aqua-vitae** alcohol
germane related	**prognostication** a weather forecast
grace the noble class	**gently considered** bribed
stoned executed by having stones	**tender** introduce
thrown at him	**effect your suits** grant your plea

CLOWN He seems to be the more noble in being fantastical. A great man, I'll warrant: I know by the picking on's teeth.

AUTOLYCUS The fardel there – what's i'th'fardel? Wherefore that box? 710

SHEPHERD Sir, there lies such secrets in this fardel and box which none must know but the king, and which he shall know within this hour, if I may come to th'speech of him.

AUTOLYCUS Age, thou hast lost thy labour.

SHEPHERD Why, sir? 715

AUTOLYCUS The king is not at the palace. He is gone aboard a new ship to purge melancholy and air himself; for, if thou be'st capable of things serious, thou must know the king is full of grief.

SHEPHERD So 'tis said, sir – about his son, that should have married a shepherd's daughter. 720

AUTOLYCUS If that shepherd be not in handfast, let him fly. The curses he shall have, the tortures he shall feel, will break the back of man, the heart of monster.

CLOWN Think you so, sir?

AUTOLYCUS Not he alone shall suffer what wit can make heavy and 725
vengeance bitter, but those that are germane to him, though removed fifty times, shall all come under the hangman; which, though it be great pity, yet it is necessary. An old sheep-whistling rogue, a ram-tender, to offer to have his daughter come into grace? Some say he shall be stoned; but that death is too soft for 730
him, say I. Draw our throne into a sheep-cote? All deaths are too few, the sharpest too easy.

CLOWN Has the old man e'er a son, sir, do you hear, an't like you, sir?

AUTOLYCUS He has a son – who shall be flayed alive; then, 'nointed over with honey, set on the head of a wasp's nest; then stand till he be 735
three-quarters and a dram dead; then recovered again with aqua-vitae or some other hot infusion; then, raw as he is, and in the hottest day prognostication proclaims, shall he be set against a brick wall, the sun looking with a southward eye upon him, where he is to behold him with flies blown to death. But what talk we of 740
these traitorly rascals, whose miseries are to be smiled at, their offences being so capital? Tell me, for you seem to be honest plain men, what you have to the king. Being something gently considered, I'll bring you where he is aboard, tender your persons to his presence, whisper him in your behalfs; and if it be in man besides 745
the king to effect your suits, here is man shall do it.

The Shepherd pays Autolycus to plead his case to the king.
The Clown promises a similar payment to Autolycus for his help.
Autolycus intends to bring them to Florizel in hope of a reward.

1 Imagery: bribing authority

In lines 748–9, the Clown suggests that he thinks men in authority can
be bribed. His image is of a bear (strong authority) being led by the
nose with gold. Think about how effective you find the image, then
suggest an image of your own that describes how people in authority
may be bribed.

2 Autolycus speaks his mind

In a soliloquy the theatrical convention is that a character speaks
truthfully. The Shepherd has paid Autolycus to take him and his son
to Polixenes, but Autolycus will take them to Florizel. Is Autolycus
genuinely concerned for his former master, or simply hoping for his
old job back as a reward? Explore ways of speaking Autolycus' soliloquy
(lines 772–80) to show an audience whether he is speaking truthfully
throughout.

3 Reviewing the scene

Identify the main episodes in Scene 4 and prepare a graph showing the
variations in tension during the action.

4 A ballad about Perdita

Write the ballad which Autolycus prepares for sale, in which he
describes the rise and fall of Perdita's fortunes.

Close agree the deal
that gold all the gold that
pawn security, pledge
moiety half
gone else ruined otherwise

look upon the hedge relieve
  myself
booties rewards, prizes
occasion opportunity
aboard him aboard Florizel's ship
matter a reward

CLOWN [*Aside to Shepherd*] He seems to be of great authority. Close
    with him, give him gold; and though authority be a stubborn bear,
    yet he is oft led by the nose with gold. Show the inside of your
    purse to the outside of his hand, and no more ado. Remember –   750
    'stoned' and 'flayed alive'.
SHEPHERD An't please you, sir, to undertake the business for us, here
    is that gold I have. I'll make it as much more, and leave this young
    man in pawn till I bring it you.
AUTOLYCUS After I have done what I promised?   755
SHEPHERD Ay, sir.
AUTOLYCUS Well, give me the moiety. [*To Clown*] Are you a party in
    this business?
CLOWN In some sort, sir; but though my case be a pitiful one, I hope
    I shall not be flayed out of it.   760
AUTOLYCUS O, that's the case of the shepherd's son. Hang him, he'll
    be made an example.
CLOWN [*To Shepherd*] Comfort, good comfort! We must to the king and
    show our strange sights. He must know 'tis none of your daughter,
    nor my sister; we are gone else. [*To Autolycus*] Sir, I will give you   765
    as much as this old man does when the business is performed, and
    remain, as he says, your pawn till it be brought you.
AUTOLYCUS I will trust you. Walk before toward the sea-side; go on the
    right hand. I will but look upon the hedge, and follow you.
CLOWN We are blest in this man, as I may say, even blest.   770
SHEPHERD Let's before, as he bids us. He was provided to do us good.

                [*Exeunt Shepherd and Clown*]

AUTOLYCUS If I had a mind to be honest, I see Fortune would not suffer
    me: she drops booties in my mouth. I am courted now with a double
    occasion: gold, and a means to do the prince my master good; which
    who knows how that may turn back to my advancement? I will bring   775
    these two moles, these blind ones, aboard him. If he think it fit to
    shore them again, and that the complaint they have to the king
    concerns him nothing, let him call me rogue for being so far
    officious; for I am proof against that title and what shame else
    belongs to't. To him will I present them; there may be matter in it.   780

                        [*Exit*]

Looking back at Act 4
Activities for groups or individuals

1 'I have served Prince Florizel'

Autolycus claims that he used to work for Prince Florizel. Invent a story telling why Florizel employed him initially, and why their relationship ended. There is a small clue in Scene 3, lines 75–7.

'A gallimaufry of gambols'. If you were directing the play what effect on the audience would you wish to achieve by your staging of the satyrs' dance?

2 Puzzles about Perdita

The only dialogue between Perdita and the Clown is in Scene 4, lines 206–10. Talk together about:

- Why did Shakespeare choose not to show more of Perdita in the company of those with whom she grew up?
- Should Perdita have some kind of 'country' accent?
- What is revealed about Perdita's character by her fears about the 'scurrilous words' (rude language) in Autolycus' songs?

'A prize, A prize!' In this staging, Autolycus quite literally descends upon the Clown.

3 The Clown

Although the script calls the Shepherd's son, the Clown, this does not mean that he is a comic figure. His description of the deaths of Antigonus and the mariners is humorous, but natural kindness leads him to return to bury Antigonus' remains. He acts as a Good Samaritan to Autolycus. Write character notes for an actor who is preparing to play the Clown. Think about mannerisms, costume, accent and stage business at particular moments during Act 4.

Cleomenes asserts that sixteen years of mourning is sufficient, but Leontes cannot forget the wrongs he did. Paulina reminds him that he killed his perfect queen. Cleomenes begs her to speak more kindly.

1 The passage of time

In Act 3 Scene 2, lines 231–9, Leontes vowed to grieve for Hermione and Mamillius as long as he lives. Sixteen years have now passed since the deaths of Leontes' wife and child.

a Suggest how you would show the effects of Leontes' 'saint-like sorrow' in the appearance of the actor. You may like to look for ideas at pages 35 and 170, where there are two photos of Leontes from the same production.

b As stage designer, work on the challenge of how the action of the play returns to Sicilia after the passage of sixteen years. For example, would you want there to be any change in the set from Act 1, or just in the appearance of the characters?

2 Opening lines

Advise the actor playing Cleomenes how he might speak lines 1–6 (despairingly? encouragingly? or …?). Also suggest what Leontes said just before the scene starts. Perhaps Leontes, Paulina and Cleomenes have come from the grave of Hermione and Mamillius. How might this affect their entry?

3 Harsh words (in pairs)

Paulina returns to the sharply critical tone that she used in the first half of the play. She reminds Leontes of his responsibility for Hermione's death with the stark word, 'killed'. Show your partner how Leontes might react to line 15, and speak his lines 16–20.

---

sorrow mourning penance
done trespass committed wrong
With them like them

My blemishes in them my faults in comparison with her virtues
heirless without an heir to the throne

ACT 5   SCENE 1
Sicilia: King Leontes' palace

Enter LEONTES, CLEOMENES, DION, PAULINA *and Servants*

CLEOMENES Sir, you have done enough, and have performed
    A saint-like sorrow. No fault could you make
    Which you have not redeemed; indeed, paid down
    More penitence than done trespass. At the last,
    Do as the heavens have done, forget your evil;   5
    With them forgive yourself.
LEONTES   Whilst I remember
    Her and her virtues, I cannot forget
    My blemishes in them, and so still think of
    The wrong I did myself, which was so much
    That heirless it hath made my kingdom and   10
    Destroyed the sweet'st companion that e'er man
    Bred his hopes out of.
PAULINA   True, too true, my lord.
    If one by one you wedded all the world,
    Or from the all that are took something good
    To make a perfect woman, she you killed   15
    Would be unparalleled.
LEONTES   I think so. Killed!
    She I killed! I did so; but thou strik'st me
    Sorely to say I did. It is as bitter
    Upon thy tongue as in my thought. Now, good now,
    Say so but seldom.
CLEOMENES   Not at all, good lady.   20
    You might have spoken a thousand things that would
    Have done the time more benefit, and graced
    Your kindness better.

Dion gives strong reasons for Leontes to marry again – to produce an heir to the throne. Paulina reminds him that the oracle said there could be no heir until Leontes' lost child was found.

1 Think of the kingdom (in groups of three)

Shakespeare's contemporary audience would have been well aware of the potential dangers of having a ruler without a child to succeed to the throne. Many of them would recall the uncertainties of the last years of Elizabeth I's reign, when no one was sure who would succeed her. When Paulina says 'Great Alexander/Left his to th'worthiest' (lines 47–8), she is thinking of Alexander the Great of Macedonia. He was held to be a model for all kings and he claimed that his successor should be 'the worthiest'. Paulina's words may also be seen as a compliment to James I, who succeeded Elizabeth on the throne of England, implying he is the worthiest successor.

Choose one or more of the following activities:

a Present a TV debate between Paulina and Dion as they argue the issue of Leontes' remarriage. Paulina is a forceful character so the person in the chair needs to be firm in ensuring fair debate.

b Write two opposing newspaper editorials on the same topic, using the arguments from the script.

c Take on the task of director and advise the actors. How might Dion and Paulina deliver their speeches in the most persuasive manner? How might Leontes react, firstly to the argument between Paulina and Dion, and then to her sensual completion of his description of a kiss, lines 54–5?

---

fail of issue lack of children
Respecting to compare with
Will have fulfilled ... purposes
will ensure that their secret plans
are carried out

tenor message, meaning
Which that it shall ... reason
this seems to our human brains as
fantastic
squared me to obeyed

PAULINA   You are one of those
              Would have him wed again.
DION   If you would not so,
              You pity not the state nor the remembrance   25
              Of his most sovereign name; consider little
              What dangers by his highness' fail of issue
              May drop upon his kingdom and devour
              Incertain lookers-on. What were more holy
              Than to rejoice the former queen is well?   30
              What holier than, for royalty's repair,
              For present comfort and for future good,
              To bless the bed of majesty again
              With a sweet fellow to't?
PAULINA   There is none worthy,
              Respecting her that's gone. Besides, the gods   35
              Will have fulfilled their secret purposes;
              For has not the divine Apollo said,
              Is't not the tenor of his oracle,
              That King Leontes shall not have an heir
              Till his lost child be found? Which that it shall   40
              Is all as monstrous to our human reason
              As my Antigonus to break his grave
              And come again to me; who, on my life,
              Did perish with the infant. 'Tis your counsel
              My lord should to the heavens be contrary,   45
              Oppose against their wills. Care not for issue;
              The crown will find an heir. Great Alexander
              Left his to th'worthiest; so his successor
              Was like to be the best.
LEONTES   Good Paulina,
              Who hast the memory of Hermione,   50
              I know, in honour, O that ever I
              Had squared me to thy counsel! Then, even now,
              I might have looked upon my queen's full eyes,
              Have taken treasure from her lips –
PAULINA   And left them
              More rich for what they yielded.

Leontes says that if he remarried, Hermione's ghost would reproach him. He thinks of Hermione's eyes as incomparable stars and promises Paulina that he will not re-marry, unless to a wife of her choosing.

'My true Paulina'. Leontes vows never to marry until Paulina bids him.

soul-vexed as a disturbed spirit	**'Remember mine'** 'Remember my
'Why to me?' 'Why do you offer	eyes' (or 'my dead children')
this insult to me?'	**Affront** appear before
incense provoke	**office** duty
rift burst	**again in breath** alive again

LEONTES   Thou speak'st truth.   55
No more such wives; therefore no wife. One worse,
And better used, would make her sainted spirit
Again possess her corpse, and on this stage,
Were we offenders now, appear soul-vexed
And begin, 'Why to me?'
PAULINA   Had she such power,   60
She had just cause.
LEONTES   She had, and would incense me
To murder her I married.
PAULINA   I should so.
Were I the ghost that walked, I'd bid you mark
Her eye and tell me for what dull part in't
You chose her; then I'd shriek, that even your ears   65
Should rift to hear me, and the words that followed
Should be 'Remember mine'.
LEONTES   Stars, stars,
And all eyes else dead coals! Fear thou no wife;
I'll have no wife, Paulina.
PAULINA   Will you swear
Never to marry but by my free leave?   70
LEONTES Never, Paulina, so be blest my spirit!
PAULINA Then, good my lords, bear witness to his oath.
CLEOMENES You tempt him over-much.
PAULINA   Unless another,
As like Hermione as is her picture,
Affront his eye.
CLEOMENES   Good madam –
PAULINA   I have done.   75
Yet if my lord will marry – if you will, sir,
Nor remedy, but you will – give me the office
To choose you a queen. She shall not be so young
As was your former, but she shall be such
As, walked your first queen's ghost, it should take joy   80
To see her in your arms.
LEONTES   My true Paulina,
We shall not marry till thou bid'st us.
PAULINA   That
Shall be when your first queen's again in breath;
Never till then.

A Servant announces the arrival of Florizel and Perdita. He says that she is the most beautiful woman he has seen. Paulina reminds him that once he had said that about Hermione.

1 The Servant's only appearance

The good news is that you have passed the audition. The bad news is that you're the Servant and this is your only appearance on stage. How will you prepare for this small role? He must be quite a trusted servant since he is able to enter without hindrance and speak immediately to Leontes. He knows Paulina well and may once have been the Court Poet (Paulina says he wrote poetry about Hermione: 'Your verse/ Flowed with her beauty once').

2 The good old days? (in small groups)

Many people believe that things were better in the past. Paulina's lines 96–7 suggest quite the opposite. What do you think?

3 'Most peerless'

The Servant praises Perdita in four of his five speeches. In lines 106–9, he describes her beauty as powerful enough to begin a new religious sect, and draw to her anyone she asked, even those who had previously followed another religion ('proselytes' are converts).

Make a list of all the words and images that the Servant uses to praise Perdita. Then invent one or two images of your own that claim her beauty is without equal.

---

gives out himself says he is called
Like to in a manner appropriate to
So out of circumstance without ceremony
framed planned
train entourage, followers

mean shabby
peerless incomparable
'tis shrewdly ebbed your opinions have changed
professors else believers in other faiths

Enter a SERVANT

SERVANT One that gives out himself Prince Florizel,   85
            Son of Polixenes, with his princess – she
            The fairest I have yet beheld – desires access
            To your high presence.
LEONTES   What with him? He comes not
            Like to his father's greatness. His approach,
            So out of circumstance and sudden, tells us   90
            'Tis not a visitation framed, but forced
            By need and accident. What train?
SERVANT   But few,
            And those but mean.
LEONTES   His princess, say you, with him?
SERVANT Ay, the most peerless piece of earth, I think,
            That e'er the sun shone bright on.
PAULINA   O Hermione,   95
            As every present time doth boast itself
            Above a better gone, so must thy grave
            Give way to what's seen now. [*To the Servant*] Sir, you
            yourself
            Have said and writ so, but your writing now
            Is colder than that theme: she had not been   100
            Nor was not to be equalled – thus your verse
            Flowed with her beauty once; 'tis shrewdly ebbed,
            To say you have seen a better.
SERVANT   Pardon, madam.
            The one I have almost forgot – your pardon –
            The other, when she has obtained your eye,   105
            Will have your tongue too. This is a creature,
            Would she begin a sect, might quench the zeal
            Of all professors else, make proselytes
            Of who she but bid follow.
PAULINA   How! Not women!
SERVANT Women will love her that she is a woman   110
            More worth than any man; men that she is
            The rarest of all women.
LEONTES   Go, Cleomenes;
            Yourself, assisted with your honoured friends,
            Bring them to our embracement.

                                        Exit [*Cleomenes with others*]

Leontes expresses his surprise at Florizel's unexpected arrival.
He comments on Florizel's likeness to Polixenes and on Perdita's beauty.
Florizel claims to bear Polixenes' greetings.

1 Still harping on fidelity

Give your response to this comment by an actor who played Leontes:
'He was a terrible king; he became jealous of the relationship between
his wife and his best friend without any evidence, he tried to corrupt
his closest adviser, he denied the truth of the oracle, neglected his
kingdom for sixteen years to carry out self-imposed penance, and after
all that, his first words to Florizel are that at least *his* mother didn't
commit adultery!'

2 Mother and daughter

Does Leontes see a resemblance between Perdita and Hermione? In
some productions the two roles are played by the same actor. Identify
a moment in Leontes' speech where he might suddenly think he sees
Hermione in Perdita.

3 'All greetings' (in pairs)

Explore ways of speaking Florizel's speech to Leontes. Speak it first as
sincerely as you can. Then try a slightly forced manner as if the speech
has only just been learned by heart. Which is more effective?

---

our prince Mamillius
Unfurnish me of reason make
  me insane
print your royal father off make
  a perfect copy of your father
hit perfectly copied
begetting wonder causing
  amazement

but infirmity, ... worn times
  were it not that the weakness that
  comes with old age
hath something seized has
  reduced
Measured crossed
the sceptres ... living all other
  living kings

                                    Still, 'tis strange
       He thus should steal upon us.
PAULINA   Had our prince,   115
       Jewel of children, seen this hour, he had paired
       Well with this lord; there was not full a month
       Between their births.
LEONTES   Prithee, no more; cease; thou know'st
       He dies to me again when talked of. Sure,
       When I shall see this gentleman, thy speeches   120
       Will bring me to consider that which may
       Unfurnish me of reason. They are come.

       Enter FLORIZEL, PERDITA, CLEOMENES, *and others*

       Your mother was most true to wedlock, prince,
       For she did print your royal father off,
       Conceiving you. Were I but twenty-one,   125
       Your father's image is so hit in you,
       His very air, that I should call you brother,
       As I did him, and speak of something wildly
       By us performed before. Most dearly welcome!
       And your fair princess – goddess! O, alas!   130
       I lost a couple that 'twixt heaven and earth
       Might thus have stood, begetting wonder, as
       You, gracious couple, do. And then I lost –
       All mine own folly – the society,
       Amity too, of your brave father, whom,   135
       Though bearing misery, I desire my life
       Once more to look on him.
FLORIZEL   By his command
       Have I here touched Sicilia, and from him
       Give you all greetings that a king, at friend,
       Can send his brother; and but infirmity,   140
       Which waits upon worn times, hath something seized
       His wished ability, he had himself
       The lands and waters 'twixt your throne and his
       Measured to look upon you, whom he loves –
       He bade me say so – more than all the sceptres   145
       And those that bear them living.

Leontes is moved to fresh guilt when he remembers how he treated Polixenes. Florizel lies to account for Perdita's presence and his lack of servants. Leontes regretfully remembers his lack of children.

1 Lies, all lies

Florizel has already told one set of lies (lines 137–46), and now he tells more. Almost every line he has spoken so far in this scene contains an untruth.

Think of a time when you may have found yourself in a similar situation of telling an increasingly complicated story to get yourself out of trouble. This may help you to sympathise with Florizel as he embroiders his story, claiming Perdita is the daughter of a warlord in Libya.

2 Dramatic irony

Leontes greets Florizel and Perdita in lines 150–1 as being as welcome as the spring. His words unconsciously foreshadow that his personal winter will be over when he discovers Perdita's true identity.

Suggest how, as director, you would highlight the dramatic irony in lines 175–7 when Leontes refers to Perdita as his wished-for lost daughter.

3 Blessings – and puzzles (in pairs)

a One person speaks Leontes' lines 167–77. The other echoes all his words connected with holiness and goodness.

b The 'father' referred to in lines 173–5 may be Polixenes or Smalus (the father that Florizel has invented for Perdita). Which father do you think Leontes has in mind? Why?

c To whom does Leontes speak 'you' (line 168): Florizel or Perdita?

---

offices,/So rarely kind representatives with their exceptionally friendly greeting
interpreters indicators
paragon perfect creature
Neptune god of the sea
adventure risk

Smalus Synalus, a Carthaginian warlord (Carthage is in Libya)
My best train most of my followers
bend to signify travel to announce
climate here stay in this region
issueless childless

LEONTES   O my brother –
          Good gentleman! – the wrongs I have done thee stir
          Afresh within me; and these thy offices,
          So rarely kind, are as interpreters
          Of my behind-hand slackness. Welcome hither,   150
          As is the spring to th'earth! And hath he too
          Exposed this paragon to th'fearful usage,
          At least ungentle, of the dreadful Neptune
          To greet a man not worth her pains, much less
          Th'adventure of her person?
FLORIZEL   Good my lord,   155
          She came from Libya.
LEONTES   Where the warlike Smalus,
          That noble honoured lord, is feared and loved?
FLORIZEL Most royal sir, from thence; from him whose daughter
          His tears proclaimed his, parting with her; thence,
          A prosperous south wind friendly, we have crossed   160
          To execute the charge my father gave me
          For visiting your highness. My best train
          I have from your Sicilian shores dismissed,
          Who for Bohemia bend to signify
          Not only my success in Libya, sir,   165
          But my arrival and my wife's in safety
          Here where we are.
LEONTES   The blessèd gods
          Purge all infection from our air whilst you
          Do climate here! You have a holy father,
          A graceful gentleman, against whose person,   170
          So sacred as it is, I have done sin;
          For which the heavens, taking angry note,
          Have left me issueless; and your father's blest,
          As he from heaven merits it, with you,
          Worthy his goodness. What might I have been,   175
          Might I a son and daughter now have looked on,
          Such goodly things as you!

*A lord announces that Polixenes has arrived and wants Florizel arrested.
Polixenes threatens the Shepherd and the Clown with tortures. Florizel
fears Camillo's betrayal and admits he has not married Perdita.*

1 Another change of mood

The report of Polixenes' arrival marks an abrupt change in the mood of
the scene. The joy celebrating the arrival of Florizel and Perdita
evaporates. The abruptness of the change in atmosphere parallels
Leontes' sudden onset of jealousy in Act 1 and Polixenes' outburst of
anger in Act 4.

If you were directing the play, how might you stage the shift in
mood?

2 Amazing news! (in pairs)

The lord cannot believe the news he has to report. His amazement
matches the surprising events: 'it becomes/My marvel and my message'.
Imagine the lord is also a freelance newspaper reporter, and phone in
your story. The other person, as editor, is full of questions.

3 'The odds for high and low's alike'

Florizel's line 206 might mean that 'there's no chance of rich and poor
marrying' *or* that 'both rich and poor have to suffer bad fortune'.
Which interpretation do you prefer? Or do you think both are equally
possible?

4 Leontes' thoughts

Leontes has only three short lines opposite. Advise the actor, with
reasons, how to speak them.

---

bear no credit not be believed
nigh near
Bohemia King Polixenes
attach arrest
seeming lady apparently noble lady

Lay't so to his charge tell him to
his face
divers deaths in death various
methods of torturing them to death

Enter a LORD

LORD   Most noble sir,
    That which I shall report will bear no credit
    Were not the proof so nigh. Please you, great sir,
    Bohemia greets you from himself by me;   180
    Desires you to attach his son, who has –
    His dignity and duty both cast off –
    Fled from his father, from his hopes, and with
    A shepherd's daughter.
LEONTES   Where's Bohemia? Speak.
LORD Here in your city; I now came from him.   185
    I speak amazedly, and it becomes
    My marvel and my message. To your court
    Whiles he was hast'ning – in the chase, it seems,
    Of this fair couple – meets he on the way
    The father of this seeming lady, and   190
    Her brother, having both their country quitted
    With this young prince.
FLORIZEL   Camillo has betrayed me,
    Whose honour and whose honesty till now
    Endured all weathers.
LORD   Lay't so to his charge:
    He's with the king your father.
LEONTES   Who? Camillo?   195
LORD Camillo, sir; I spake with him, who now
    Has these poor men in question. Never saw I
    Wretches so quake. They kneel, they kiss the earth,
    Forswear themselves as often as they speak.
    Bohemia stops his ears and threatens them   200
    With divers deaths in death.
PERDITA   O my poor father!
    The heaven sets spies upon us, will not have
    Our contract celebrated.
LEONTES   You are married?
FLORIZEL We are not, sir, nor are we like to be.
    The stars, I see, will kiss the valleys first: 205
    The odds for high and low's alike.

Florizel admits that Perdita is not a princess. Leontes wishes Perdita could be his. Paulina rebukes him. Leontes agrees to plead with Polixenes on behalf of Florizel and Perdita.

1 Recognition? (in pairs)

Leontes feels affectionate towards Perdita and hints that he recognises Hermione in her (lines 226–7). Does Paulina's rebuke suggest that she has realised who Perdita is? If Paulina has recognised Perdita it makes it even more important that she steer Leontes away from Perdita. Whether or not she has recognised Perdita will affect the way she says lines 223–6. Try speaking the lines both ways and suggest how each might affect the audience's perception of the dramatic irony of her words.

2 Leontes agrees to help

When Leontes hears that Florizel has lied to him he appears unlikely to support Perdita and Florizel. But within a few lines he has agreed to help them. Is it the sight of Perdita which moves him, even though he considers her 'not so rich in worth (social status) as beauty'? Or is it Florizel's appeal to think of his own feelings when he was young? Or might there be another reason? If you were playing Leontes, how long a dramatic pause at line 228 would you have before you agree?

3 Forecast

Before you read on, predict what you imagine will be the result of the meeting between Camillo, Leontes, Polixenes, Florizel and Perdita.

---

visible an enemy obviously an enemy
since you owed ... now when you were the same age as me
Step forth come forward as

Your honour ... desires if your emotions have not led you into dishonourable actions
mark what way see what success

LEONTES   My lord,
　　　Is this the daughter of a king?
FLORIZEL   She is,
　　　When once she is my wife.
LEONTES   That 'once' I see by your good father's speed
　　　Will come on very slowly. I am sorry,   210
　　　Most sorry, you have broken from his liking,
　　　Where you were tied in duty; and as sorry
　　　Your choice is not so rich in worth as beauty,
　　　That you might well enjoy her.
FLORIZEL   Dear, look up.
　　　Though Fortune, visible an enemy,   215
　　　Should chase us with my father, power no jot
　　　Hath she to change our loves. Beseech you, sir,
　　　Remember since you owed no more to time
　　　Than I do now. With thought of such affections,
　　　Step forth mine advocate; at your request   220
　　　My father will grant precious things as trifles.
LEONTES   Would he do so, I'd beg your precious mistress,
　　　Which he counts but a trifle.
PAULINA   Sir, my liege,
　　　Your eye hath too much youth in't. Not a month
　　　'Fore your queen died she was more worth such gazes   225
　　　Than what you look on now.
LEONTES   I thought of her
　　　Even in these looks I made. But your petition
　　　Is yet unanswered. I will to your father.
　　　Your honour not o'erthrown by your desires,
　　　I am friend to them and you; upon which errand   230
　　　I now go toward him. Therefore follow me,
　　　And mark what way I make. Come, good my lord.

                                              Exeunt

The First Gentleman describes the opening of the bundle, the Shepherd's story of the baby, and Leontes' and Camillo's meeting. The Second Gentleman says Leontes' daughter is found, the oracle fulfilled.

1 Characterisation (in groups of three)

The three Gentlemen speak only in lines 1–89 when they report the off-stage action in which Leontes is reunited with his long-lost daughter and all the reconciliations that follow. Actors playing the Gentlemen create characters so that their acting is not one-dimensional. Take parts as the Gentlemen and speak lines 1–89 (ignore Autolycus' lines). Then work on your chosen character by writing notes about his personality. The differences in the language they use can help you. The First Gentleman moves from simple description to much more formal language. Rogero (Second Gentleman) says little in spite of being questioned. He hasn't actually seen anything of the meeting but is keen to be involved. The Third Gentleman is obviously excited and is very voluble. He feels he can't do justice to the story in his retelling of the events.

2 'The oracle is fulfilled'

The king's daughter has been found after sixteen years and Leontes has an heir to his throne. The Second Gentleman uses a vivid image to describe the celebrations: 'Nothing but bonfires'. (Bonfires have traditionally been a popular way of celebrating a national event.)

a Compose a ballad or poem in celebration of the discovery.

b Imagine Leontes commissions a work of art to celebrate the event. Submit your designs.

c Write the newspaper headlines for various papers of different types (broadsheet, tabloid) which report the event.

---

this relation the telling of what happened
fardel bundle
issue outcome
broken delivery disjointed report

very notes of admiration indeed signs of wonder
happily perhaps
verity truth

ACT 5   SCENE 2
Sicilia: near Leontes' palace

Enter AUTOLYCUS, *and a* GENTLEMAN

AUTOLYCUS Beseech you, sir, were you present at this relation?

1 GENTLEMAN I was by at the opening of the fardel, heard the old
shepherd deliver the manner how he found it; whereupon, after a
little amazedness, we were all commanded out of the chamber.
Only this methought I heard the shepherd say: he found the child.   5

AUTOLYCUS I would most gladly know the issue of it.

1 GENTLEMAN I make a broken delivery of the business, but the
changes I perceived in the king and Camillo were very notes of
admiration. They seemed almost, with staring on one another, to
tear the cases of their eyes. There was speech in their dumbness,   10
language in their very gesture; they looked as they had heard of a
world ransomed, or one destroyed. A notable passion of wonder
appeared in them; but the wisest beholder that knew no more but
seeing could not say if th'importance were joy or sorrow – but in
the extremity of the one it must needs be.   15

Enter another GENTLEMAN

Here comes a gentleman that happily knows more. The news,
Rogero?

2 GENTLEMAN Nothing but bonfires. The oracle is fulfilled: the king's
daughter is found. Such a deal of wonder is broken out within this
hour that ballad-makers cannot be able to express it.   20

Enter another GENTLEMAN

Here comes the Lady Paulina's steward; he can deliver you more.
How goes it now, sir? This news, which is called true, is so like an
old tale that the verity of it is in strong suspicion. Has the king
found his heir?

The Third Gentleman reports that Perdita was proved the king's daughter. Leontes, torn by conflicting emotions, asked Polixenes' forgiveness. Paulina grieved for Antigonus but rejoiced in Perdita.

1 Shakespeare explains his staging

Shakespeare chooses not to show the scene where father and daughter are re-united. Instead, he has the events recounted by the Three Gentlemen. Why? Write the speech in which Shakespeare gives the actors his reasons why he is not going to show Leontes' meeting with Perdita but use this 'reporting' method.

2 Act it out (in small groups)

Stage the discovery of Perdita and the other events as a dumb show (mime), using some of the Gentlemen's lines 2–46 as narration.

3 'Lames report', 'undoes description'

In lines 45–6, the Third Gentleman is so overwhelmed by the scene he has witnessed that he feels anything he says to describe the occasion will not do justice to it ('which lames report'). In *Antony and Cleopatra*, Enobarbus uses a similar phrase when trying to describe Cleopatra: 'For her own person,/It beggared all description'.

Think of other phrases you might use for someone lost for words in this sort of situation.

4 Paulina's words to Perdita

For sixteen years Paulina has had faith that the oracle would be fulfilled and Perdita would be found. Speak lines 57–62 ('But O ...'), then write the first words which you imagine Paulina spoke to Perdita.

---

pregnant by circumstance made convincing by evidence
mantle cloak
character handwriting
affection quality
favour facial features
clipping embracing

conduit water channel
matter to ... credit be asleep a story to tell though not believed
avouches swears
innocence simplicity
bark ship

3 GENTLEMAN Most true, if ever truth were pregnant by circumstance.   25
That which you hear you'll swear you see, there is such unity in the
proofs: the mantle of Queen Hermione's; her jewel about the neck
of it; the letters of Antigonus found with it, which they know to be
his character; the majesty of the creature in resemblance of the
mother; the affection of nobleness which nature shows above her   30
breeding, and many other evidences proclaim her with all certainty
to be the king's daughter. Did you see the meeting of the two kings?
2 GENTLEMAN No.
3 GENTLEMAN Then have you lost a sight which was to be seen, cannot
be spoken of. There might you have beheld one joy crown another,   35
so and in such manner that it seemed sorrow wept to take leave of
them, for their joy waded in tears. There was casting up of eyes,
holding up of hands, with countenance of such distraction that they
were to be known by garment, not by favour. Our king, being ready
to leap out of himself for joy of his found daughter, as if that joy were   40
now become a loss cries 'O, thy mother, thy mother!'; then asks
Bohemia forgiveness; then embraces his son-in-law; then again
worries he his daughter with clipping her; now he thanks the old
shepherd, which stands by like a weather-bitten conduit of many
kings' reigns. I never heard of such another encounter, which lames   45
report to follow it and undoes description to do it.
2 GENTLEMAN What, pray you, became of Antigonus, that carried
hence the child?
3 GENTLEMAN Like an old tale still, which will have matter to rehearse
though credit be asleep and not an ear open: he was torn to pieces   50
with a bear. This avouches the shepherd's son, who has not only
his innocence, which seems much, to justify him but a handkerchief
and rings of his that Paulina knows.
1 GENTLEMAN What became of his bark and his followers?
3 GENTLEMAN Wracked the same instant of their master's death, and in   55
the view of the shepherd; so that all the instruments which aided to
expose the child were even then lost when it was found. But O the
noble combat that 'twixt joy and sorrow was fought in Paulina! She
had one eye declined for the loss of her husband, another elevated
that the oracle was fulfilled. She lifted the princess from the earth   60
and so locks her in embracing as if she would pin her to her heart,
that she might no more be in danger of losing.

*The Third Gentleman relates how Perdita wept at Leontes' tale of
Hermione's death. Everyone is going with Paulina to see a newly
completed statue of Hermione. Autolycus claims credit for the discoveries.*

1 'That rare Italian master'

Julio Romano was a real artist (Giulio Romano 1499–1546), famous for
painting and architecture rather than for sculpture. Among his claims
to fame were a series of erotic etchings which were considered so
obscene that the Pope kept them from public view in his private
library. Shakespeare may have found a clue in Romano's epitaph:
'painted statues breathed ... by virtue of Julio'.

Speak the Third Gentleman's lines 75–82 to express the excitement
and wonder he feels at having such news to tell.

2 Autolycus the listener? (in small groups)

Autolycus has not spoken since his two lines at the beginning of the
scene. What has he been doing? Advise the actor about how to behave
between lines 7–89.

3 Autolycus' story

The sea-sickness suffered by Florizel and Perdita prevented them
from listening carefully to Autolycus' story about the Shepherd and
the fardel. Write a short speech for Autolycus to deliver to Florizel, in
hope of some reward for his efforts.

---

angled fished
attentiveness wounded
 listening pained
dolour grief
fain almost
marble hard hearted
performed completed
rare talented

beguile Nature of her custom
 do Nature out of her job
ape mimic
thence absent
unthrifty to our knowledge lose
 the opportunity to know more
preferment promotion
relished found a place

1 GENTLEMAN The dignity of this act was worth the audience of kings and princes, for by such was it acted.

3 GENTLEMAN One of the prettiest touches of all, and that which angled for mine eyes – caught the water though not the fish – was, when at the relation of the queen's death, with the manner how she came to't bravely confessed and lamented by the king, how attentiveness wounded his daughter, till from one sign of dolour to another she did, with an 'Alas!', I would fain say bleed tears; for I am sure my heart wept blood. Who was most marble there changed colour; some swooned, all sorrowed. If all the world could have seen't, the woe had been universal.

1 GENTLEMAN Are they returned to the court?

3 GENTLEMAN No. The princess, hearing of her mother's statue, which is in the keeping of Paulina – a piece many years in doing and now newly performed by that rare Italian master, Julio Romano, who, had he himself eternity and could put breath into his work, would beguile Nature of her custom, so perfectly he is her ape. He so near to Hermione hath done Hermione that they say one would speak to her and stand in hope of answer. Thither with all greediness of affection are they gone, and there they intend to sup.

2 GENTLEMAN I thought she had some great matter there in hand, for she hath privately twice or thrice a day ever since the death of Hermione visited that removed house. Shall we thither, and with our company piece the rejoicing?

1 GENTLEMAN Who would be thence that has the benefit of access? Every wink of an eye some new grace will be born. Our absence makes us unthrifty to our knowledge. Let's along.

Exeunt [Gentlemen]

AUTOLYCUS Now, had I not the dash of my former life in me, would preferment drop on my head. I brought the old man and his son aboard the prince, told him I heard them talk of a fardel and I know not what; but he at that time overfond of the shepherd's daughter – so he then took her to be – who began to be much sea-sick, and himself little better, extremity of weather continuing, this mystery remained undiscovered. But 'tis all one to me; for had I been the finder-out of this secret, it would not have relished among my other discredits.

*The Shepherd and Clown are delighted with their new clothes and status.
They tell Autolycus that they are now gentlemen. He asks them to put in
a good word for him with Florizel.*

1 'Gentleman born' (in groups of three)

The seven mentions of 'gentleman born' in lines 102–11 may in part be
Shakespeare's private joke. He seems to have been conscious of social
status, and with the money he earned from his success as a playwright
bought his father a coat of arms, so making him a 'gentleman'.

a Do you think that clothes are important in making others accept
  you? Talk together about what you think makes a 'lady' or a
  'gentleman' and whether perhaps Shakespeare is making the point
  that in his instinctive willingness to adopt Perdita, the Shepherd
  is indeed a 'gentleman born'.

b Take parts as Autolycus, the Shepherd and the Clown, and
  rehearse trying to come to terms with your new situation (lines
  99–142). Remember that the comedy comes from the words, so
  make your actions bring out the sense, and nonsense, of the
  language.

2 Lottery winners (in small groups)

Use this episode to prepare a short play showing the effects on a group
of people of a large lottery win. They wish to become 'gentlemen' or
'gentlewomen'. How might they treat former colleagues or bosses for
example?

---

blossoms of their fortune
  expensive new clothes

preposterous prosperous
  (the Clown mistakes his words)
gentle kind and courteous

Enter SHEPHERD *and* CLOWN

Here come those I have done good to against my will, and already
appearing in the blossoms of their fortune.   100
SHEPHERD   Come, boy, I am past moe children, but thy sons and
daughters will be all gentlemen born.
CLOWN   [*To Autolycus*] You are well met, sir. You denied to fight with
me this other day because I was no gentleman born. See you these
clothes? Say you see them not and think me still no gentleman   105
born. You were best say these robes are not gentleman born. Give
me the lie, do, and try whether I am not now a gentleman born.
AUTOLYCUS   I know you are now, sir, a gentleman born.
CLOWN   Ay, and have been so any time these four hours.
SHEPHERD   And so have I, boy.   110
CLOWN   So you have; but I was a gentleman born before my father, for the
king's son took me by the hand and called me brother, and then the
two kings called my father brother, and then the prince my brother
and the princess my sister called my father father, and so we wept;
and there was the first gentleman-like tears that ever we shed.   115
SHEPHERD   We may live, son, to shed many more.
CLOWN   Ay, or else 'twere hard luck, being in so preposterous estate as
we are.
AUTOLYCUS   I humbly beseech you, sir, to pardon me all the faults I
have committed to your worship and to give me your good report   120
to the prince my master.
SHEPHERD   Prithee, son, do; for we must be gentle now we are
gentlemen.
CLOWN   Thou wilt amend thy life?
AUTOLYCUS   Ay, and it like your good worship.   125

The Clown says that now he is a gentleman he can lie, and therefore promises to swear that Autolycus is honest, brave and sober. Leontes and the others visit Paulina to see Hermione's statue.

1 Serious or comic? ... or both?

The Clown offers to help Autolycus. He claims that a gentleman can tell any lie to help a friend. Do you think that Shakespeare is using lines 126–37 to comment on the morality of the nobility of his time, or is his intention only to make the audience laugh?

2 Change in fortunes

How does Autolycus feel about the rise in fortunes of the Shepherd and Clown? What does he think of the Clown's offer of assistance, and the description of his courage, 'a tall fellow of thy hands'? Step into role as Autolycus and write a final soliloquy for him to speak, giving his view on all that has happened, and what he thinks now of the Clown and the Shepherd.

3 Scene change

After the comedy, the location changes, but a lengthy set change would interrupt the flow of the action, and make it difficult for the actors to create the necessary tension for the last scene of the play. In Paulina's house, there must be a curtain which can be drawn aside, and sufficient space for the whole court. As set designer solve this problem of the rapid change of scene.

---

boors peasants
franklins middle-class people (freeholders)
tall fellow of thy hands brave man in a fight
the queen's picture Hermione's effigy, statue

grave dignified
paid home repaid in full
vouchsafed graciously agreed
contracted/Heirs betrothed inheritors (Florizel and Perdita)

CLOWN Give me thy hand. I will swear to the prince thou art as honest
a true fellow as any is in Bohemia.

SHEPHERD You may say it, but not swear it.

CLOWN Not swear it, now I am a gentleman? Let boors and franklins
say it; I'll swear it.   130

SHEPHERD How if it be false, son?

CLOWN If it be ne'er so false, a true gentleman may swear it in the
behalf of his friend; [*To Autolycus*] and I'll swear to the prince
thou art a tall fellow of thy hands, and that thou wilt not be drunk;
but I know thou art no tall fellow of thy hands, and that thou wilt   135
be drunk. But I'll swear it, and I would thou wouldst be a tall
fellow of thy hands.

AUTOLYCUS I will prove so, sir, to my power.

CLOWN Ay, by any means prove a tall fellow. If I do not wonder how
thou dar'st venture to be drunk, not being a tall fellow, trust me   140
not. Hark, the kings and the princes, our kindred, are going to see
the queen's picture. Come, follow us; we'll be thy good masters.

Exeunt

ACT 5 SCENE 3
Sicilia: Paulina's house

Enter LEONTES, POLIXENES, FLORIZEL, PERDITA, CAMILLO,
PAULINA, LORDS and Attendants

LEONTES O grave and good Paulina, the great comfort
That I have had of thee!

PAULINA   What, sovereign sir,
I did not well, I meant well. All my services
You have paid home. But that you have vouchsafed,
With your crowned brother and these your contracted   5
Heirs of your kingdoms, my poor house to visit,
It is a surplus of your grace, which never
My life may last to answer.

Leontes asks Paulina to show him the statue of Hermione.
Paulina replies that she keeps it separate from her other art treasures.
She draws the curtain to show the statue.

---

1 'I like your silence' (in large groups)

In every production the unveiling of Hermione's statue is always a thrilling moment. Lines 21–2 suggest that everyone stands silent, wondering at the life-like appearance of the statue. Create a tableau of the scene where the statue is revealed. Ask members of other groups to identify the major characters in your frozen picture.

2 Humour – or not? (in pairs)

It is easy for the actor playing Leontes to get a laugh from the audience on lines 28–9 ('not so much wrinkled'), and even easier for Polixenes with his line, 'O not by much!'.

Try several ways of speaking the lines, for example, trying to achieve the most comical effect, then trying to make it as poignant as possible. Talk together about which you feel would be the most effective in performance on stage. Compare your ideas with other pairs.

---

singularities rare treasures
peerless without an equal

lively mocked realistically imitated
not chiding lack of criticism

LEONTES   O Paulina,
        We honour you with trouble. But we came
        To see the statue of our queen. Your gallery   10
        Have we passed through, not without much content
        In many singularities; but we saw not
        That which my daughter came to look upon,
        The statue of her mother.
PAULINA   As she lived peerless,
        So her dead likeness I do well believe   15
        Excels whatever yet you looked upon,
        Or hand of man hath done; therefore I keep it
        Lonely, apart. But here it is. Prepare
        To see the life as lively mocked as ever
        Still sleep mocked death. Behold, and say 'tis well!   20

        [*Paulina draws a curtain and reveals Hermione, as a statue*]

        I like your silence; it the more shows off
        Your wonder. But yet speak; first you, my liege.
        Comes it not something near?
LEONTES   Her natural posture!
        Chide me, dear stone, that I may say indeed
        Thou art Hermione; or rather thou art she   25
        In thy not chiding, for she was as tender
        As infancy and grace. But yet, Paulina,
        Hermione was not so much wrinkled, nothing
        So agèd as this seems.
POLIXENES   O not by much!

Leontes is moved by the life-like statue and recalls his courtship of Hermione. Perdita wishes to kiss the hand of the statue but Paulina prevents her. Camillo and Polixenes try to comfort Leontes.

1 Shared line, shared feelings? (in pairs)

The appearance of the statue affects all those present. Leontes feels ashamed that the statue seems to express more feeling than he can. Perdita kneels, wishing for blessing from what she thinks is the stone figure of her mother.

Because Perdita shares line 42 with Leontes and begins her speech with 'And', it may seem almost a continuation of her father's words. Talk together whether you think father and daughter are experiencing the same emotions at this moment.

2 Unspoken emotion

Leontes does not speak between lines 42 and 59, yet Camillo, Polixenes and Paulina all comment on his grief. What would you suggest that the actor playing Leontes does during this time to justify their response to him?

3 Theatrical magic (in small groups)

Take parts as Leontes and Perdita. Read aloud lines 34–46 while the rest of the group echo all the words which refer to magic, love, life and death.

What audience response would you wish to evoke here?

4 Is Polixenes 'the cause'

What do Polixenes' lines 53–6 suggest about his character? He offers to take much of Leontes' grief upon himself, and sees himself responsible for Hermione's death. Is he really 'the cause' of all the unhappiness in the play as he seems to suggest?

---

royal piece noble work of art
conjured to remembrance
  magically restored to my memory
took the spirits taken breath

but newly fixed only recently
  painted
too sore laid on too severely felt
piece up in take upon
wrought affected, moved

PAULINA   So much the more our carver's excellence,   30
        Which lets go by some sixteen years and makes her
        As she lived now.

LEONTES   As now she might have done,
        So much to my good comfort as it is
        Now piercing to my soul. O thus she stood,
        Even with such life of majesty – warm life,   35
        As now it coldly stands – when first I wooed her.
        I am ashamed. Does not the stone rebuke me
        For being more stone than it? O royal piece!
        There's magic in thy majesty, which has
        My evils conjured to remembrance and   40
        From thy admiring daughter took the spirits,
        Standing like stone with thee.

PERDITA   And give me leave,
        And do not say 'tis superstition, that
        I kneel and then implore her blessing. Lady,
        Dear queen, that ended when I but began,   45
        Give me that hand of yours to kiss.

PAULINA   O, patience!
        The statue is but newly fixed, the colour's
        Not dry.

CAMILLO   My lord, your sorrow was too sore laid on,
        Which sixteen winters cannot blow away,   50
        So many summers dry. Scarce any joy
        Did ever so long live; no sorrow
        But killed itself much sooner.

POLIXENES   Dear my brother,
         Let him that was the cause of this have power
        To take off so much grief from you as he   55
        Will piece up in himself.

PAULINA   Indeed, my lord,
         If I had thought the sight of my poor image
        Would thus have wrought you – for the stone is mine –
        I'd not have showed it.

LEONTES   Do not draw the curtain.

PAULINA   No longer shall you gaze on't, lest your fancy   60
        May think anon it moves.

Leontes thinks that Hermione's statue seems to breathe. He wishes to kiss it but Paulina prevents him. She promises to make the statue come down and take Leontes by the hand.

'I'll make the statue move indeed'. Compare this illustration with a different staging of the same moment shown on page 203.

fixure colour and setting	**forbear** stop
so far transported so carried away	**Quit presently** leave immediately
settled senses normal mind	**can behold it** are able to bear the
cordial comfort heart-warming	sight
medicine	

LEONTES   Let be, let be!
  Would I were dead, but that methinks already.
  What was he that did make it? See, my lord,
  Would you not deem it breathed, and that those veins
  Did verily bear blood?
POLIXENES   Masterly done!   65
  The very life seems warm upon her lip.
LEONTES The fixure of her eye has motion in't,
  As we are mocked with art.
PAULINA   I'll draw the curtain:
  My lord's almost so far transported that
  He'll think anon it lives.
LEONTES   O sweet Paulina,   70
  Make me to think so twenty years together!
  No settled senses of the world can match
  The pleasure of that madness. Let't alone.
PAULINA I am sorry, sir, I have thus far stirred you; but
  I could afflict you farther.
LEONTES   Do, Paulina,   75
  For this affliction has a taste as sweet
  As any cordial comfort. Still methinks
  There is an air comes from her. What fine chisel
  Could ever yet cut breath? Let no man mock me,
  For I will kiss her.
PAULINA   Good my lord, forbear.   80
  The ruddiness upon her lip is wet:
  You'll mar it if you kiss it, stain your own
  With oily painting. Shall I draw the curtain?
LEONTES No, not these twenty years.
PERDITA   So long could I
  Stand by, a looker-on.
PAULINA   Either forbear,   85
  Quit presently the chapel, or resolve you
  For more amazement. If you can behold it,
  I'll make the statue move indeed, descend,
  And take you by the hand. But then you'll think –
  Which I protest against – I am assisted   90
  By wicked powers.

Paulina says her magic is lawful and calls for music to waken the statue.
Hermione descends and embraces Leontes who is amazed to feel her
warm flesh. Paulina tells Hermione that Perdita is found.

The statue's thoughts

The actor playing Hermione has to stand perfectly still for a long time.
Read Edwin Morgan's poem 'Instructions to an Actor', below (which
continues on page 200), then write an interior monologue of the
thoughts you might have if you were playing Hermione, standing
stockstill as the statue.

Now, boy, remember this is the great scene.
You'll stand on a pedestal behind a curtain,
the curtain will be drawn, and then you don't move
for eighty lines; don't move, don't speak, don't breathe.
I'll stun them all out there. I'll scare them,
make them weep, but it depends on you.
I warn you eighty lines is a long time,
but you don't breathe, you're dead,
you're a dead queen, a statue,
you're dead as stone, new carved,
new-painted, and the paint not dry
– we'll get some red to keep your lip shining –
and you're a mature woman, you've got dignity,
some beauty still in middle age, and
you're kind and true, but you're dead,
your husband thinks you're dead,
the audience thinks you're dead,
and you don't breathe, boy, I say
you don't even blink for eighty lines,
if you blink you're out!
Fix your eye on something and keep watching it.
Practise when you get home. It can be done.
And you move at last – music's the cue.
When you hear a mysterious solemn jangle
of instruments, make yourself ready.
Five lines more, you can lift a hand.
It may tingle a bit, but lift it –
slow, slow –
O this is where I hit them
right between the eyes, I've got them now –
I'm making the dead walk –

LEONTES   What you can make her do
I am content to look on, what to speak
I am content to hear; for 'tis as easy
To make her speak as move.
PAULINA   It is required
You do awake your faith. Then all stand still;   95
On: those that think it is unlawful business
I am about, let them depart.
LEONTES   Proceed.
No foot shall stir.
PAULINA   Music; awake her; strike.

                    [*Music*]

'Tis time; descend; be stone no more; approach;
Strike all that look upon with marvel. Come;   100
I'll fill your grave up. Stir; nay, come away;
Bequeath to death your numbness, for from him
Dear life redeems you.
[*Hermione moves, and begins to descend*]
                          You perceive she stirs.
Start not: her actions shall be holy as
You hear my spell is lawful. [*To Leontes*] Do not shun her   105
Until you see her die again, for then
You kill her double. Nay, present your hand:
When she was young you wooed her; now, in age,
Is she become the suitor?
LEONTES   O, she's warm!
If this be magic, let it be an art   110
Lawful as eating.
POLIXENES   She embraces him.
CAMILLO She hangs about his neck.
If she pertain to life, let her speak too.
POLIXENES Ay, and make it manifest where she has lived,
Or how stol'n from the dead.
PAULINA   That she is living,   115
Were it but told you, should be hooted at
Like an old tale; but it appears she lives,
Though yet she speak not. Mark a little while.
[*To Perdita*] Please you to interpose, fair madam; kneel,
And pray your mother's blessing. Turn, good lady: 120
Our Perdita is found.

Hermione says that she kept herself alive in order to see her daughter, Perdita. Leontes suggests that Camillo and Paulina should marry. He asks Polixenes and Hermione for their forgiveness.

'Instructions to an Actor' by Edwin Morgan, continued from page 198

> you move a foot, slow, steady, down,
> you guard your balance in case you're stiff,
> you move, you step down, down from the pedestal,
> control your skirt with one hand, the other hand
> you now hold out –
> O this will melt their hearts if nothing does –
> to your husband who wronged you long ago
> and hesitates in amazement
> to believe you are alive.
> Finally he embraces you, and there's nothing
> I can give you to say, boy,
> but you must show that you have forgiven him.
> Forgiveness, that's the thing. It's like a second life.
> I know you can do it. – Right then, shall we try?

Stage the scene (in groups of six or more)

Scene 3 ends the play with memorable dramatic action: the revealing of the statue, Hermione's descent, Leontes' reaction, and the final reconciliations. Take parts and stage the scene, thinking especially about:

- How will Hermione 'unfreeze' from statue to living woman at line 103?
- How does Leontes say 'O, she's warm!'?
- Why is Perdita silent from line 85 to the end of the play?
- Why does Hermione speak only to Perdita and not to Leontes?
- What feelings do you hope the audience will have at the end of your performance?
- How might you stage the final departures to express the reconciliations that have taken place?
- What will be the final image your audience will see as the lights fade?

---

sacred vials holy vessels
thou wast in being you were living
upon this push at this moment
trouble interrupt
like relation similar stories

turtle turtle dove (see page 122, and page 212 Activity e)
till I am lost until I die
troth-plight betrothed, engaged
dissevered parted

HERMIONE   You gods, look down,
 And from your sacred vials pour your graces
 Upon my daughter's head! Tell me, mine own,
 Where hast thou been preserved? Where lived? How found
 Thy father's court? For thou shalt hear that I,   125
 Knowing by Paulina that the oracle
 Gave hope thou wast in being, have preserved
 Myself to see the issue.
PAULINA   There's time enough for that,
 Lest they desire upon this push to trouble
 Your joys with like relation. Go together,   130
 You precious winners all; your exultation
 Partake to every one. I, an old turtle,
 Will wing me to some withered bough, and there
 My mate, that's never to be found again,
 Lament till I am lost.
LEONTES   O peace, Paulina!   135
 Thou shouldst a husband take by my consent,
 As I by thine a wife. This is a match,
 And made between's by vows. Thou hast found mine –
 But how is to be questioned, for I saw her
 As I thought dead, and have in vain said many   140
 A prayer upon her grave. I'll not seek far –
 For him, I partly know his mind – to find thee
 An honourable husband. Come, Camillo,
 And take her by the hand, whose worth and honesty
 Is richly noted, and here justified   145
 By us, a pair of kings. Let's from this place.
 [*To Hermione*] What! Look upon my brother. Both your
  pardons,
 That e'er I put between your holy looks
 My ill suspicion. This your son-in-law,
 And son unto the king, whom, heavens directing,   150
 Is troth-plight to your daughter. Good Paulina,
 Lead us from hence, where we may leisurely
 Each one demand and answer to his part
 Performed in this wide gap of time since first
 We were dissevered. Hastily lead away.   155

           Exeunt

Looking back at the play

Activities for groups or individuals

1 Picky critics

Over the centuries various criticisms have been levelled at *The Winter's Tale*. These include:

- the suddenness of Leontes' jealousy
- the abrupt change of tone in the middle of Act 3 scene 3
- the chance meeting of Florizel and Perdita
- the apparent confusion over Florizel's clothes
- the sixteen-year gap
- the irrelevance of Autolycus to the main plot
- Bohemia's sea coast (Bohemia is landlocked)
- the manner of Antigonus' death
- the off-stage discovery of Perdita's identity
- the statue scene.

Write a defence of *The Winter's Tale* justifying the dramatic effectiveness of as many of these points as you can.

2 Lost and found

During the course of the play, each major character loses something precious, but eventually finds either what they lost, or something equally valued. Step into role as each major character and tell what you have lost and found.

3 Autolycus remembers

What did Autolycus do next? Write the account published by a tabloid newspaper when Autolycus is interviewed. He describes what he remembers of the events in the play, and then tells of his next escapade, after the play ended.

4 Fairytale or Christian drama?

Use the information given on pages 204, 206 and 209 to help you organise a debate on: '*The Winter's Tale* is a fairytale told through drama, not a religious drama'.

5 Hermione's point of view …

Tell the story of *The Winter's Tale* in role as Hermione. Does she think that her marriage can return to the same basis of trust as before Leontes' onset of jealousy? Do you?

6 A great gap of time

After her 're-birth' Hermione speaks only to Perdita. Continue the conversation as mother and daughter catch up on the missed sixteen years.

7 A spiritual journey

Make a time chart to show significant stages in the spiritual journey made by either Leontes or Hermione.

'What fine chisel/Could ever yet cut breath?' Compare this staging of the statue scene with the illustration on page 196.

Shakespeare's Late Plays

The Winter's Tale, *The Tempest*, *Cymbeline* and *Pericles* are generally referred to as Shakespeare's Late Plays. Almost certainly the first three are the last plays which Shakespeare wrote without a collaborator. Seven years after his death, Shakespeare's fellow actors, Heminges and Condell, published the First Folio (see page 220). They grouped Shakespeare's plays under the headings of Histories, Tragedies and Comedies. They placed *The Winter's Tale* and *The Tempest* in the Comedies and *Cymbeline* in the Tragedies; *Pericles* they omitted altogether. More than a hundred years ago, critics began to feel that these four late plays did not fit comfortably within the Folio categories.

The Winter's Tale is a confusing play for those who like to categorise. It's not a tragedy, though it has tragic elements. On the other hand, though it ends in reconciliation and harmony, the deaths of Antigonus and the innocent Mamillius prevent the easy definition of comedy. Much of the plot is logically incredible.

Many critics argue that the four late plays share several characteristics which suggest they should be grouped together. Such critics call these plays *Romances* and identify their common features as:

- a child who is lost and is found again
- an important character who is a young woman closely linked with the theme of regeneration and rebirth, and with chastity
- mythical and fantastic plots, involving the apparently dead coming to life, magical events, storms, exotic locations and long distances travelled
- an ending which suggests a sense of restoration and renewal – a potential for good
- varied and flexible image and language patterns
- many more lines shared between characters (see pages 136 and 215)
- a three-part structure, consisting of a potentially tragic opening, a gap of time for growth and learning, and a resolution which does not depend entirely on the actions of the characters but on magic or chance. (In *The Tempest*, the first two parts have already happened and are narrated by Prospero.)

Make your own summary of these features of Romances and identify an example of each in *The Winter's Tale*.

What is *The Winter's Tale* about?

There can be no single assessment of what *The Winter's Tale* is about. The title of the play is significant. If it were called *A Winter's Tale*, it would imply that it is just a story to help pass a long winter's evening. *The Winter's Tale* implies that Shakespeare has universal ideas in mind: the effects of winter, both the season in Nature and the chilling results of Leontes' jealousy.

One way of answering the question, 'What is *The Winter's Tale* about?' is to identify the themes of the play. Some of the themes are introduced below.

The destructive nature of jealousy

Leontes' jealousy is sparked by what he thinks is a double betrayal – by his wife, and by the friend whom he calls his brother. Jealousy is a common experience and is still the subject of novels and even of popular songs today. Leontes ultimately recognises its devastating effects:

'The wrong I did myself, which was so much
That heirless it hath made my kingdom and
Destroyed the sweet'st companion ...' (Act 5 Scene 1, lines 9–11)

Repentance and regeneration

Hearing of the death of his son and his wife, Leontes' mad jealousy changes to deep sorrow and repentance. He vows to spend the rest of his life grieving over their dead bodies as an act of repentance for his folly: 'Come, and lead me/To these sorrows.' (Act 3 Scene 2, lines 239–40).

After the winter of Leontes' jealousy in Sicilia, regeneration occurs in Bohemia's spring. Death is conquered by apparent rebirth, and Leontes' wife and daughter live again. Perdita refers to the Greek myth of Proserpina (which tells how winter turns to spring, see page 120). The connection of this myth to Perdita herself is made explicit when she and Florizel are welcomed by Leontes: 'As is the spring to th'earth!'. (Act 5 Scene 1, line 151)

Perhaps the most striking expression of the theme of regeneration is Paulina's command to the statue to:

'descend; be stone no more; approach;
Strike all that look upon with marvel. Come;
I'll fill your grave up.' (Act 5 Scene 3, lines 99–101)

Nature and art

In Act 4 Scene 4, Perdita and Polixenes discuss whether human beings should interfere with Nature (by grafting new varieties of plants). Polixenes argues that Nature's 'art' (natural processes and instincts) is superior to the 'art' (action) of humans:

'so over that art,
Which you say adds to nature, is an art
That nature makes.' (Act 4 Scene 4, lines 90–2)

Throughout the play, the need is shown for people to work with nature and not against it. To do otherwise can be destructive. Antigonus takes the unnatural step of exposing the baby Perdita to the elements and is killed. Leontes behaves unnaturally, so losing his son Mamillius, and sixteen years of life with his wife and daughter. Florizel follows the natural feelings of his heart and is eventually rewarded with a wife. The Shepherd and his son also follow their instincts. Their care for Perdita shows their natural nobility of character.

Faith and religion

Those who believe that *The Winter's Tale* is a specifically Christian play point to the long period of Leontes' atonement and the 'resurrection' of Hermione. It is certainly a play full of religious overtones, culminating in Paulina's: 'It is required/You do awake your faith.' (Act 5 Scene 3, lines 94–5)

Cleomenes and Dion stress the holiness of the oracle by describing, in Act 3 Scene 1, the reverence that they felt at the shrine. Hermione appeals to the gods at her trial and is steadfast in her faith for sixteen years, as she finally looks upon her long-lost daughter, Perdita:

'Knowing by Paulina that the oracle
Gave hope thou wast in being, have preserved
Myself to see the issue.' (Act 5 Scene 3, lines 126–8)

The strength and fidelity of women

All three major female characters show great courage and faithfulness. Hermione bravely defends herself at her trial, constant in the knowledge of her innocence. Perdita is unafraid of Polixenes' threats. Paulina boldly stands up to Leontes in her steadfast defence of Hermione, and she remains loyal, not only to her queen, but also to the tyrant king who acknowledges his debt:

> 'O grave and good Paulina, the great comfort
> That I have had of thee!' (Act 5 Scene 3, lines 1–2)

Sexuality

Polixenes' lines suggest that he thinks that the awareness of sexuality corrupted both his and Leontes' childhood innocence:

> 'Had we pursued that life,
> And our weak spirits ne'er been higher reared
> With stronger blood, we should have answered heaven
> Boldly, "Not guilty", the imposition cleared
> Hereditary ours.' (Act 1 Scene 2, lines 71–5)

And he specifically blames the temptation of women for his fall from grace:

> 'O my most sacred lady,
> Temptations have since then been born to's' (Act 1 Scene 2, lines 76–7)

Leontes' jealousy provokes him to believe that all women are sexually unfaithful. His imagery expresses his paranoia about women's sexual infidelity:

> 'she has been sluiced in's absence,
> And his pond fished by his next neighbour' (Act 1 Scene 2, lines 194–5)

Joy and celebration

The play opens with Archidamus and Camillo discussing the celebration of the friendship between Leontes and Polixenes through feasting. Much of the second half of the play takes place at the pastoral feast that crowns the sheep-shearing festival in Bohemia. And the wonder and rejoicing that takes place in Sicilia when Perdita returns to her father are vividly conveyed in the Second Gentleman's description: 'Nothing but bonfires.' (Act 5 Scene 2, line 18)

Time

Time concerns Shakespeare intensely in *The Winter's Tale*. He even includes a character called Time, who might be thought of as a forerunner of the theatre programme, designed to help the audience follow the story. One production took this view and shared Time's lines (Act 4 Scene 1) between the cast. Florizel and Perdita spoke the words about themselves; some characters were busy using make-up to age their appearance; others held objects connected with time, such as an hourglass and scythe.

At the end of the first half of the play, Shakespeare presents several traditional ways of picturing time. For example, the ship-wrecking storm might be seen as Shakespeare's pun on tempest (Latin: *tempus*, time). The bear which kills Antigonus may represent the movement of time, disrupting the action of a romance story. The Shepherd finds the baby, Perdita. This image of the old man and the young child is still used today in many countries to represent the end of the old year and the beginning of the new. There are many indications throughout the play that time is at work. Act 1 Scene 2 is full of references to time: 'Nine changes of the wat'ry star' (line 1); 'a jar o'th'clock' (line 43); Polixenes seems to feel that time has been destructive of innocence, when he speaks of the past (lines 62–80). Leontes, rushing headlong towards insane jealousy, speaks in erratic, unrhythmical verse which underlines his maddened feelings:

> 'Wishing clocks more swift?
> Hours, minutes? Noon, midnight?' (lines 289–90)

By the end of the play, after a sixteen-year wait, Leontes has gained a son, through the marriage of the daughter that time has restored to him. In Act 4 Scene 4, lines 79–82, Perdita uses strikingly varied time imagery as she relates her flowers to the seasons of the year:

> 'Sir, the year growing ancient,
> Not yet on summer's death nor on the birth
> Of trembling winter, the fairest flowers o'th'season
> Are our carnations and streaked gillyvors'

Shakespeare often gives a clue to a major theme of each of his plays in the opening scene. Turn to the conversation between Achidamus and Camillo, Act 1 Scene 1 from line 30 to the end of the scene. Identify references to age and youth, life and death, and the hope that time contains.

Telling the tale

One production of *The Winter's Tale* began with a group of actors seated at a fireside. They spoke the first 32 lines of Act 2 as a prologue and their costumes were in a different style from the rest of the production. This reinforced the idea that the whole play is a 'winter's tale' of regeneration after a bleak season of hatred.

Throughout the play references to the idea of a tale resonate:
'A sad tale's best for winter' (Act 2, Scene 1, line 25)
'so like an old tale' (Act 5 Scene 2, lines 22–3)
'Like an old tale still' (Act 5 Scene 2, line 49)
'hooted at/Like an old tale' (Act 5 Scene 3, lines 116–17)
At the start of Act 4, Time speaks of the story as 'my tale' (line 14). Such descriptions suggest that the audience is not meant to interpret the play as a representation of everyday reality but to recognise that *The Winter's Tale* has the psychological reality of myth.

As the tale draws to its compelling end, one of the Gentlemen says that, 'Such a deal of wonder is broken out within this hour that balladmakers cannot be able to express it.' (Act 5 Scene 2, lines 19–20). His words are a dramatically ironic echo of the exaggerated ballads described earlier by Autolycus.

Shakespeare's inspiration for *The Winter's Tale* was a popular contemporary story, Robert Greene's *Pandosto* (1588), which is subtitled *The Triumph of Time*. He follows Greene's tale closely but changes and elaborates it to produce a far more moving dramatic work. For example Shakespeare:
• intensifies the irrationality of Leontes' jealousy
• invents the roles of Paulina and Autolycus
• restores Hermione to life (in *Pandosto*, the Queen dies).
In *Pandosto*, the King lusts after the girl whom he does not yet know is his daughter. On learning the truth he kills himself.

a Talk together about what you understand by the idea of 'the tale'. How might you use it when staging *The Winter's Tale*?

b Rewrite *The Winter's Tale* as a folk or fairy story, using as many story-telling conventions as possible, for example, 'Once upon a time there was a king …'.

Women in *The Winter's Tale*

The Winter's Tale is unusual amongst Shakespeare's plays in having three strongly defined roles for women. Originally these parts would all have been taken by boys. It is also unusual in that none of the women resorts to dressing in male attire to achieve their ends. In these aspects it is probably closest to *All's Well That Ends Well*.

Male attitudes to women are clear: women are the equivalent of property, 'Whiles other men have gates ...' (Act 1 Scene 2, line 197), and are untrustworthy if not strictly controlled. It is not only Leontes who thinks like this. Antigonus vows to castrate his daughters if Hermione is proved unfaithful. Polixenes threatens to disfigure Perdita, accusing her of attracting Florizel by witchcraft.

Hermione

Hermione is a challenging role for any actor because her character needs to be established strongly in the first half of the play. The actor spends the last part of Act 3, the whole of Act 4 and much of Act 5 in her dressing room, only appearing as the statue at the end of Act 5 where she is the focus of the action yet has only a single speech.

At the beginning of the play, Hermione is pregnant with her second child and seems full of joy. Her teasing of Polixenes borders on the flirtatious. Their conversation about the innocence of childhood exposes men's double standards towards women; for Polixenes, Hermione is both 'sacred' and a 'temptation'.

Her language with Mamillius in Act 2 suggests the normal irritation of a heavily pregnant mother with an importunate child. It is short-lived and they settle down for a delightful exchange where the child wishes to entertain his mother secretly, 'yon crickets shall not hear it', with a tale of 'sprites and goblins'. These images of Hermione contrast strongly with the irrational and violent jealousy of Leontes.

At her trial Hermione can call no witnesses in her defence. She is rushed 'to this place, i'th'open air', like a common criminal to be publicly vilified. Hermione remains regal remembering that, 'The Emperor of Russia was my father'. She defends herself by saying that she loved Polixenes 'With such a kind of love as might become/A lady like me' (Act 3 Scene 2, lines 62–3).

Paulina

Paulina seems to occupy the position normally reserved in Shakespeare for the Fool. She appears licensed to say what she feels to Leontes. Although he threatens her with various tortures he is unable to silence her. She is the source of humour in Act 2 Scene 3 from her entrance into the presence of the king when Leontes says to Antigonus, 'I charged thee that she should not come about me./I knew she would' (lines 43–4), to her independent exit, 'So, so; farewell, we are gone' (line 129).

Paulina is courageous. When threatened by Leontes with death by burning, she retorts, 'It is an heretic that makes the fire,/Not she which burns in't' (Act 2 Scene 3, lines 114–15). Leontes' threat is one which a modern audience might not take too seriously, but in earlier days women were burnt for defying male authority. Bravely, she is the author of the plot to conceal Hermione.

From left to right: Emilia, Hermione, Paulina. Suggest what impression on the audience you think the director is trying to achieve here.

In Act 5, Paulina appears to have replaced Camillo as Leontes' chief councillor. For a woman to hold such an important office of state was virtually unknown at this time, either in drama or in real life. She is also the director of the resolution and restoration of harmony, rejecting any notion that she is 'assisted/By wicked powers' (Act 5 Scene 3, lines 90–1).

Perdita

Perdita is much more than a mere symbol of spring and renewal. Her down-to-earth individuality of character is depicted in her language. When Florizel teases her about her intention to cover him with flowers, she accepts the sexuality inherent in her love for him: 'Not like a corse; or if, not to be buried,/But quick and in mine arms' (Act 4 Scene 4, lines 131–2). Perdita's dignity and natural grace are described by Florizel in his speech beginning, 'What you do/Still betters what is done ...' (Act 4 Scene 4, lines 135–46) and is also demonstrated by her modesty and quiet demeanour in Act 5 Scene 3 when she is re-united with her mother.

Activities on women in the play

a How would you answer a critic who said: 'The play is about Leontes. Hermione is merely a catalyst to provoke a reaction from him.'?

b Words like 'sacred', 'precious' and 'grace' are frequently associated with Hermione. Use a dictionary to list as many definitions as can you find for 'grace'. Decide how the different meanings illuminate your understanding of Hermione. Talk together about how far the different meanings of 'grace' affect your thoughts about the themes of The Winter's Tale.

c Step into role as Paulina and give your motives for hiding Hermione.

d If you were directing a production of The Winter's Tale, what would you hope to achieve by having the same actor play both Hermione and Perdita?

e At the very end of the play, Paulina says she will fly like a turtle dove and roost on a dead branch grieving for Antigonus (turtle doves were popularly supposed to mate for life, see page 122). Camillo seems to have confided something to Leontes (line 142) about his feelings, but how does Paulina feel about the marriage imposed on her? Step into role as Paulina and speak her thoughts.

f 'She has no character; she is merely a plot device.' Argue against the critic who made this comment about Perdita.

g Take on the role of a strongly committed feminist who is about to direct a production of *The Winter's Tale*. Write the speech you will make to the cast when they meet for the first time.

The Winter's Tale was chosen (with *Henry V*) to open the first season of Shakespeare's plays at the re-built Globe Theatre on London's Bankside in 1997. The illustration shows Perdita at the sheep-shearing festival.

The language of *The Winter's Tale*

Imagery

The play is rich in imagery: the use of emotionally charged words and phrases which conjure up vivid mental pictures in the imagination. Shakespeare uses images drawn from all aspects of the natural and social world. For example, in a single speech (Act 1 Scene 2, lines 179–207), Leontes employs imagery of fishing, swans, demonology, theatre and acting, burial rites, property ownership, medicine, cosmology (stars and planets), warfare, travel and disease.

One significant cluster of images is that of disease and healing. As Leontes' imagination sickens, the imagery of disease infests the language of Act 1 Scene 2:

'be cured/Of this diseased opinion' (lines 296–7)
'Were my wife's liver/Infected as her life' (lines 304–5)
'There is a sickness/Which puts some of us in distemper, but/I cannot name the disease, and it is caught/Of you …' (lines 384–7)
'O then my best blood turn/To an infected jelly' (lines 417–18).

In *The Winter's Tale*, the power to heal and restore belongs to youth. Camillo says that Mamillius 'physics the subject, makes old hearts fresh' (Act 1 Scene 1, lines 31–2), Polixenes says that his son 'cures in me/Thoughts that would thick my blood' (Act 1 Scene 2, lines 170–1). The return of Perdita fulfils the oracle, helps to heal Leontes' grief, and restores life to Hermione.

Blank verse

Approximately three-quarters of the play is in blank (unrhymed) verse. Each line has five alternating unstressed (x) and stressed (/) syllables (iambic pentameter). Try tapping out the rhythm:

```
x   /   x   / x   /   x  /   x  /
```
I'll make the statue move indeed, descend (Act 5 Scene 3, line 88)

Choose a passage of about ten lines and practise speaking it in different ways to experience the underlying rhythm. Don't worry if you find that the rhythm is not exactly regular. By the time he wrote the late plays Shakespeare had moved far beyond writing blank verse in precise or unvarying rhythm.

Verse and prose

In Shakespeare's time, there were certain conventions about when to use verse or prose in a play. For example, servants and comic characters would usually speak in prose and the high-status characters in verse. Shakespeare was never afraid to break convention when it suited the situation and sometimes gave verse to a lower-class character. For example, when the Shepherd is speaking to upper-class characters he uses verse.

In Act 4 Scene 4, there is much switching from verse to prose. Turn to a few pages at random and suggest why the changes occur. One example is lines 702–3. It seems as if the Shepherd unwittingly speaks a line of verse, so the disguised Autolycus completes a rhyming couplet for him – maybe mocking the old man.

SHEPHERD   None, sir; I have no pheasant, cock nor hen.

AUTOLYCUS How blest are we that are not simple men!

Shared lines

Very often a line of verse is shared between two people.

LEONTES   For thou set'st on thy wife.

ANTIGONUS   I did not, sir.

(Act 2 Scene 3, line 141)

Such sharing of lines probably occurs more frequently in *The Winter's Tale* than any other Shakespeare play. There is a theatrical convention that when a line is shared there is no pause between speakers, indicating a sense of urgency. But is the convention always valid? Might dramatic effect be increased if actors paused in shared lines? Explore the shared line above, using each method. Do you feel a pause, or no pause, is more appropriate? See also pages 136, 138 and 194.

Rhyme

There are very few rhymed lines in the play. Most occur in the songs and in Time's speech, which is written entirely in rhyming couplets. It has been suggested that Time's speech is not Shakespeare's work or that it is not an example of his best writing. One critic described it as 'doggerel'. It certainly stands out from the rest of the play, but perhaps this was Shakespeare's intention, to draw attention to Time as a figure outside the play, whose function is to tell the story of the previous sixteen years as quickly as possible. In *Pericles*, Gower fulfils a similar story-telling function.

The jealousy of Leontes

Leontes experiences jealousy even more dramatically and irrationally than Othello. 'Nothing', is a word he repeats obsessively with unconscious irony (Act 1 Scene 2, lines 284–96) when he speaks of his conviction that Hermione has betrayed him with Polixenes. His jealousy becomes all-consuming and destructive. Leontes re-defines reality to agree with his diseased imagination. As king, he has the power to enforce his definition on others. He tries to infect his courtiers with his own emotional disorder, commanding Camillo to kill Polixenes, and bidding Antigonus to take his baby daughter to be 'consumed with fire'. He rejects the holy oracle which declares that Hermione is innocent.

In almost every word Leontes hears and speaks he finds a double meaning which confirms his belief. In Act 1 Scene 2, lines 179–207, his obsession with the idea of Hermione's infidelity runs through his language. The very rhythm of his speech is affected; it becomes fractured and repetitive. Even gestures are significant to him, 'How she holds up the neb, the bill to him!'.

Two problems facing all directors of *The Winter's Tale* are the motivation and rapid onset of Leontes' jealousy. One production had Leontes' suspicions acted out under a blue light. He watched a flickering, slow-motion mime of lust between Hermione and Polixenes. They danced slowly towards each other swaying suggestively, and kissed passionately. During the mime Leontes spoke his lines agitatedly. When the lights changed again, their behaviour became normal and it was clear that their lust was only in Leontes' imagination. Another production showed Leontes' insane jealousy beginning when Hermione invited Polixenes to feel the child kicking within her womb.

Only the deaths of his son and queen bring Leontes to realise the enormity of his conduct. If *The Winter's Tale* were a tragedy, the deaths in Act 3 would be the end of the play. But Shakespeare had left tragedy behind him. The charity of the Shepherd preserves the life of Perdita, and Paulina's courage and faith lead to the fulfilment of the oracle.

- How would you stage the beginning of Leontes' jealousy to make it credible?

Designing *The Winter's Tale*

The Winter's Tale is an inviting challenge for any designer because in performance it often seems to be a play divided into two very different halves: Sicilia and Bohemia. There are also special design opportunities in the scenes involving the trial, the Bear, and Hermione's statue. Some designers establish a very strong contrast between the court in Sicilia and the pastoral scenes in Bohemia. Others try to maintain some kind of thematic link throughout the whole play.

Imagine that you are the designer of a production of *The Winter's Tale*. Choose one of the following and prepare your design notebook.

- Use colour in costume, stage design or lighting to emphasise certain emotions in the play.
- Emphasise the difference in status of the court and country scenes through your design.
- You have been given a free hand to design *The Winter's Tale* in any way that seems appropriate to you.
- *Either* redesign the cover of this edition of *The Winter's Tale*, *or* produce a poster advertising your production of the play.

Suggest what effects you think the designer and director are attempting to achieve in this staging of the opening moments of the play.

Critics' forum

The Winter's Tale has received a mixed reception from critics, directors and reviewers. Some feel that Shakespeare's creative powers were failing. Others see a mature writer unafraid to experiment with dramatic form, even at this stage of his career. Use the following comments to explore your own responses. Remember, you don't have to agree with any view if you can justify your own interpretation.

Its purpose, its lesson, is to teach forgiveness of wrongs, not vengeance for them; to give the sinner time to repent and amend, not to cut him off in his sin; to frustrate the crimes he has purposed.

  F. J. Furnivall, 1877

[The play] ... has all the fascination of a daring experiment, devised by the subtlest of artists in extending the domain of his art ... a genuine diptych in construction. It is made up of two plays, the first a tragedy and the second a comedy, so jointed in the middle as to produce a final result that belongs equally to each ... an experiment in dramatic art, may fairly be regarded as among the boldest and most conspicuous feats of his genius.

  Thomas R. Price, 1890

The Winter's Tale is a typically romantic drama, a 'winter's dream, when nights are longest', constructed in defiance of probabilities, which it rides over happily. It has all the license and it has all the charm of a fairy tale, while the matters of which it treats are often serious enough, ready to become tragic at any moment, and with much of real tragedy in them as it is.

  The principal charm in *The Winter's Tale*, its real power over the sources of delight, lies in the two women, true mother and daughter, whose fortunes we see at certain moments, the really important crises of their lives ...The end, certainly, is reconciliation, mercy – mercy extended even to the unworthy, in a spirit of something more than mere justice.

  Arthur Symons, 1890

Leontes is in a destructive nightmare, 'performed' in a 'wide gap of time'. Spring breaks through the grip of winter, love returns, enabling Leontes to awake his faith and be redeemed. Shakespeare absolves the gods of our failure; the responsibility is in us, the faith demanded is faith in ourselves.

Trevor Nunn, 1969

Trevor Nunn pompously interprets this popular nonsense as some profound allegory about a search for love through suffering and ultimate redemption. I suggest the Bard would have had hilarious hysterics at such an interpretation.

Milton Schulman, 1969

I believe the resolution and forgiveness and the happy ending are extremely fragile. I don't say it isn't going to go on but it needs more work ... There are some things you've got to forget in order to relive. 'Hastily lead away' – Why does he want to go hastily? Why does he, as the king, ask others to lead? Also it's not a rhyming couplet. It is a suspended end .... It's a question mark.

Peter Hall, 1989

The fact that Hermione never speaks to Leontes in the final scene has often seemed disturbing. But ... what *could* she possibly say? What she does offer Leontes, before they embrace is both easier and more important than words. Once again the Emperor of Russia's daughter takes the hand of the Sicilian king. The contract this time is initiated by her. It is also made (as it was not before) in perfect silence ... Hermione's voiceless hand – tendered and accepted – seals a promise for the future, and a full consent.

Anne Barton, 1994

Judged by realistic standards, the [statue] episode in *The Winter's Tale* is absurd ... But by this stage in the play we know we are not watching realistic drama, and if we have accepted the conventions in which the play is written, and responded to its poetry of both language and action, we shall experience this scene as the inevitable if unexpected conclusion of all that has gone before.

Stanley Wells, 1994

William Shakespeare 1564–1616

1564 Born Stratford-upon-Avon, eldest son of John and Mary Shakespeare.
1582 Marries Anne Hathaway of Shottery, near Stratford.
1583 Daughter, Susanna, born.
1585 Twins, son and daughter, Hamnet and Judith, born.
1592 First mention of Shakespeare in London. Robert Greene, another playwright, described Shakespeare as 'an upstart crow beautified with our feathers ...'. Greene seems to have been jealous of Shakespeare. He mocked Shakespeare's name, calling him 'the only Shake-scene in a country' (presumably because Shakespeare was writing successful plays).
1595 A shareholder in 'The Lord Chamberlain's Men', an acting company that became extremely popular.
1596 Son Hamnet dies, aged eleven.
     Father, John, granted arms (acknowledged as a gentleman).
1597 Buys New Place, the grandest house in Stratford.
1598 Acts in Ben Jonson's *Every Man in His Humour.*
1599 Globe Theatre opens on Bankside. Performances in the open air.
1601 Father, John, dies.
1603 James I grants Shakespeare's company a royal patent: 'The Lord Chamberlain's Men' became 'The King's Men' and played about twelve performances each year at court.
1607 Daughter, Susanna, marries Dr John Hall.
1608 Mother, Mary, dies.
1609 'The King's Men' begin performing indoors at Blackfriars Theatre.
1610 Probably returned from London to live in Stratford.
1616 Daughter, Judith, marries Thomas Quiney.
     Dies. Buried in Holy Trinity Church, Stratford-upon-Avon.

The plays and poems
(no one knows exactly when he wrote each play)

1589–1595 *The Two Gentlemen of Verona, The Taming of the Shrew, First, Second and Third Parts of King Henry VI, Titus Andronicus, King Richard III, The Comedy of Errors, Love's Labour's Lost, A Midsummer Night's Dream, Romeo and Juliet, King Richard II* (and the long poems *Venus and Adonis* and *The Rape of Lucrece*).

1596–1599 *King John, The Merchant of Venice, First and Second Parts of King Henry IV, The Merry Wives of Windsor, Much Ado About Nothing, King Henry V, Julius Caesar* (and probably the *Sonnets*).

1600–1605 *As You Like It, Hamlet, Twelfth Night, Troilus and Cressida, Measure for Measure, Othello, All's Well That Ends Well, Timon of Athens, King Lear.*

1606–1611 *Macbeth, Antony and Cleopatra, Pericles, Coriolanus, The Winter's Tale, Cymbeline, The Tempest.*

1613 *King Henry VIII, The Two Noble Kinsmen* (both probably with John Fletcher).

1623 Shakespeare's plays published as a collection (now called the First Folio).